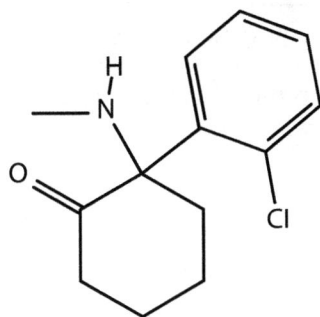

ALSO BY LEAH BENSON

Emotional Utopia; Stop Searching for Happiness and Start Living It

The Feel Good Formula®, A Personal Development Course

THE BEGINNER'S GUIDE TO

KETAMINE THERAPY
for mental health

LEAH BENSON, LMHC, Ed.M.

Forward by Kazi "Zayn" Hassan, M.D.

Published by Leah Benson, Tampa, Florida, in 2025
First edition published 2023. Second edition published 2025.

ISBN: 979-8-9874201-2-6
LCCN: 2022923241

Cover and book design by Amy Gindhart.
Author photograph by Robert Sargent.

This publication is designed to provide accurate and authoritative information in regard to the subject matter covered. It is sold with the understanding that neither the publisher nor the author is engaged in rendering medical advice. Prior to commencing any medical regime, consult your healthcare provider. Additionally, nothing contained in this book is intended to encourage or support illegal behavior. It should not be construed as advocacy for the current use of psychedelic substances outside areas where their use is legally sanctioned.

Printed in the United States of America

To my parents, who raised me to have
a love of learning and a core of skepticism.

The ordinary

waking consciousness is a very useful one,
and on most occasions, an indispensable
state of mind; but it is by no means the
only form of consciousness, nor in all
circumstances the best...

The mystical experience

is doubly valuable; it is valuable
because it gives the experiencer a
better understanding of himself and
the world and because it may help
him lead a less self-centered and
more creative life.

Aldous Huxley (1894-1963), Collected Essays

Contents

i FOREWORD

vii INTRODUCTION

Chapter 1
1 THE CASE FOR KETAMINE-ASSISTED THERAPY

Chapter 2
15 WHO STANDS TO BENEFIT FROM KETAMINE-ASSISTED THERAPY?

Chapter 3
39 WHAT TO EXPECT ON YOUR KETAMINE JOURNEY

Chapter 4
53 TRAVEL ALERT: CAVEATS AND CONTRADICTIONS

Chapter 5
69 KETAMINE AND YOUR REAL LIFE

85 ACKNOWLEDGMENTS

89 GLOSSARY

97 NOTES

103 BIBLIOGRAPHY

KETAMINE: A NEAR PERFECT ANESTHETIC. Its safety profile on the respiratory and cardiovascular systems plus its analgesic (pain-relieving) properties have made ketamine the most commonly used anesthetic in the world.

Through the serendipity of science and medicine, ketamine's rapid acting antidepressant effects were discovered.

Ketamine's journey from synthesis as an anesthetic in 1962 to its first randomized double-blinded clinical trial for depression took about 38 years.

It proved successful in helping a population of patients who had failed multiple prior medications—"treatment-resistant," these patients are called. Now, dozens of randomized double-blinded controlled trials have unequivocally demonstrated ketamine's power as an antidepressant and several studies speak to its anxiolytic (anxiety-relieving) properties.

Presently, Yale Department of Psychiatry touts the medicine as the biggest breakthrough in psychiatry in the past 50 years, which speaks to the incredible evolution of a chemical first described as a dissociative anesthetic; today contentiously classified as a true psychedelic.

As the current psychedelic renaissance began to unfold in the early 2000s, IV ketamine clinics emerged alongside efforts by non-profits like the Multidisciplinary Association for Psychedelic Studies, (MAPS). MAPS uses MDMA to treat Post Traumatic Stress Disorder (PTSD) in veterans and first-responders in Phase 3 clinical trials seeking FDA approval. Academic institutions like Johns Hopkins are testing psilocybin as a treatment for existential anxiety in life-threatening cancer.

The popularity of ketamine clinics grew rapidly. However, many of the clinics' directing physicians viewed ketamine simply as a pharmacological tool without context or appreciation for its psychedelic properties. They administered the treatment multiple times a week, following the protocol of the well-controlled clinical trials using sub-anesthetic doses for treatment-resistant depression.

Since then, the industry has become psychedelically informed. Knowledge that the impact of ketamine is deeply influenced by the set and setting of the experience, and awareness that this directly affects the treatments' effectiveness and durability (how long the relief lasts) is now prevalent.

Companies like Field Trip Health and Nushama have created aspirational environments in which patients experience the therapy, but these come at a cost unattainable to many, as insurance reimbursement is atypical and most patients pay cash.

From synthesis as an anesthetic to acceptance as a psychiatric intervention by the National Institute of Mental Health and American Psychiatric Association, ketamine's value continues to expand. Its latest value being that of facilitating the birth of a true art form, Ketamine Assisted Psychotherapy, (KAP).

This use of ketamine in no way invalidates its medicinal application. Its neurobiological effects are indeed powerful and have given researchers incredible insights into the mechanisms of depression. Ronald Duman et al. of Yale psychiatry have published extensively on ketamine's ability to induce neuroplasticity, reduce neuroinflammation, and modulate network activity to treat depression, anxiety and PTSD.

Ketamine's story took another pivot during the COVID-19 pandemic. In the face of a severe mental health and supply chain crisis, regulators responded by legislating a waiver to the Ryan-Haight act. This well intentioned regulation prohibited the prescription of controlled substances through telemedicine in an attempt to maintain a standard of care when dealing with opiates for pain management, but the law's application to schedule 3 controlled substances included ketamine.

Due to the Public Health Emergency waiver, telemedicine prescriptions of ketamine became possible. Companies like Mindbloom and My Ketamine Home emerged to fill the void of treating patients in the comfort and accessibility of their homes, with prescriptions of compounded tablets of ketamine mailed to their homes and self-administered after appropriate education and supervision.

As of late 2022, two large studies of those patients have demonstrated that ketamine can indeed be safely prescribed through telemedicine and self-administered at home while still being highly effective in treating treatment-resistant depression and anxiety.

Nue Life Health, a public benefits corporation, acquired My Ketamine Home in 2021 and has treated several thousand patients using its HIPAA compliant digital platform, which tracks data on each experience. The platform also curates playlists to accompany a patient's intention, and monitors their depression, anxiety and PTSD symptoms.

In addition to its current offerings, Nue Life Health continues to innovate digital tools for the patient journey, and just as importantly, tools for providers so that traditional healthcare providers like your primary care doctor may offer these clinical ketamine programs to their patients.

Finally, pioneers like Dr. Philip Wolfson recognized the growing need for education of a new generation of medical providers and therapists to learn and innovate on the best practices of working with altered states and the potential to soften and reorganize the mind through psychedelic transformation. Dr. Wolfson, having contributed the seminal work in the field with The Ketamine Papers, 2016, founded the Ketamine Training Center and continues to teach through experiential trainings in Catskill, NY and Scotts Valley, CA.

The rapid evolution of ketamine from dissociative anesthetic to the most important breakthrough in psychiatry in the last 50 years concurrent with the psychedelic renaissance captured the imagination of classically trained therapists like Leah Benson, whom I've had the honor of working with to develop the proper container for such important experiences. Leah Benson has merged her classical training with the somatic based theories of trauma in a way that is uniquely powerful when used to integrate the ketamine experience and harness its full therapeutic potential. Leah has a gift for translating science into clinical practice, and I believe this book accomplishes just that. As Leah and I have discovered in treating dozens of patients together, ketamine without integration therapy is a missed opportunity with a high chance of relapse.

Kazi "Zayn" Hassan, M.D.

CO-FOUNDER I CHIEF MEDICAL OFFICER
Nue.life
November 2022

introduction

Several years ago, my patients started asking
me about ketamine (sounds like "keh-tuh-meen")
and psychedelic-assisted psychotherapy.
I didn't have a clue... That's all changed.

Since 2020, I have been in overdrive to build my expertise in the subject. At this point, I've worked with dozens of clients using ketamine to elevate their emotional status quo, developed the integration program of one of the fastest growing ketamine startups in the country, and most importantly, methodically built my own experiential knowledge of ketamine and psychedelic-assisted therapy.

Coming from a background in what is called "depth psychology" at the beginning of my career, in 2013 I moved into body-based psychotherapy because it had become clear that for therapy to be effective, the body has to be involved.

My book Emotional Utopia is all about how that works. And it DOES work.

There are times, though, when even bigger guns are required, for depth or speed. That's where ketamine and psychedelics shine. Ketamine in particular is especially helpful for those who are not comfortable with intense feelings in their bodies.

FIRST AND FOREMOST, you need to know that "doing drugs" is not something I take lightly. I'm a cautious person. I never "took drugs," and I thought people who did were mostly irresponsible losers, or at least struggling addicts. (I was one type of casualty of the War on Drugs).

Understanding the way different "drugs" work—and how they can be effective in making people's lives better—has changed all that.

Rather than make this book about both ketamine and psychedelic-assisted therapy, I opted to focus on ketamine. Mostly because ketamine's mechanism of action and subjective experience is so different from that of traditional psychedelics—those being LSD, psilocybin, mescaline, DMT, and ayahuasca. (Not to mention the myriad of other mind-altering substances being used for mental health: MDMA, Ibogaine, and 2C-B, among many others.) For that reason, ketamine deserves its own book. Also, ketamine is currently the only "psychedelic" that is legal across the nation, so we're not in any gray areas when discussing its use. (Remember, I'm a cautious person).

The important thing for you to know about **KETAMINE VERSUS TRADITIONAL PSYCHEDELICS** is that a ketamine experience is a much gentler experience physically, even at very high doses. The fact that the molecule is an anesthetic practically assures that gentler experience, even if subjectively you begin to wonder or worry while under its influence.

Ketamine is a serious treatment for mental health concerns, and deserves to be treated as such. To make the material extremely accessible, however, I designed this book to flow as an informal conversation you and I are having in my consulting room. Try not to be fooled by my casual tone, though. There is nothing casual about this material.

Our conversation begins with the basics of ketamine, ketamine therapy, and safety. That's because I'm cautious, and because the drug war gave ketamine a bad reputation as dangerous—which it isn't. In Chapter Two I'll answer questions to help you decide if ketamine might be right for you. Chapter Three is about what to expect if you decide to take the leap. Chapter Four contains warnings and contraindications. Chapter Five will illustrate the practical changes ketamine can help create in your daily life. After that comes a glossary of terms you'll probably run across as you research this whole topic of psychedelics. A lot of the terms are pretty vague, as are the definitions out there. I've tried to make them very concrete to give you an idea of what these terms mean in a practical sense for everyday life. Lastly, I've added endnotes and a bibliography, in case you want to read more about the subject.

REST ASSURED, I am not selling ketamine or psychedelics. My business is therapy and coaching. You'll see the term "integration" all over the place when it comes to responsible ketamine and psychedelic journeying. Therapy and coaching are versions of the "integration" of ketamine and psychedelic journeys that lead to the lasting change and the elevated emotional status quo you're looking for. Therapy and coaching are not the only ways to integrate, but they're good ones. No bias here!

I'll end with a warning that I repeat ad nauseam. Ketamine and psychedelics are not a panacea. **THEY ARE A CATALYST FOR LASTING CHANGE.** If you use them for symptom management—which you can absolutely do—then that's all you'll get. If you use them as a springboard to the practice of new thought patterns and new behaviors, you'll get lasting results. These lasting results are, of course, best facilitated by a systematic self-paced program like The Feel Good Formula® I created, or by regular meetings with a therapist, coach, mentor, or guide, individually or in a group setting.

Good journey and safe travels.

Leah Benson
October 2022

chapter 1

The Case for Ketamine-Assisted Therapy

" Ketamine is not for everyone. Not everyone responds.
Not everyone finds it an easy medicine. For some,
there are immediate awakenings.
For most, it takes time for effects to manifest.
In the moment of its influence and often afterwards,
it may well be the most profound internal experience of mind. "

Phil Wolfson, M.D., in The Ketamine Papers

What is ketamine-assisted therapy?

IN SHORT, KETAMINE-ASSISTED THERAPY IS A TURBOCHARGED METHOD OF REACHING YOUR MENTAL HEALTH GOALS. This starts with turbocharging self-awareness. And why do we need self-awareness? You've no doubt heard the cliché that goes a little something like, "The first step in solving a problem is to become aware that you have a problem in the first place." Until we know exactly what our issues are, we can't begin to go about actually solving those issues—let alone moving on to building a happier, healthier life. If lasting, sustainable happiness is what you're after, gaining self-awareness is the best first step you can take.

No one with any experience in "traditional" talk therapy is going to be surprised to hear that gaining valuable self-awareness takes time—and therefore money. It's unfortunate but true: You can spend years or decades working with a competent therapist before reaching the one insight that finally unlocks the door(s) you've been banging your head against.

On the other hand, it's been my experience with patients that one ketamine session provides roughly the value of 10 regular therapy sessions. You might see ads for ketamine home-dosing programs with claims like, "Ketamine equals three years of therapy in three hours." That's just nonsense, because frequency and duration of new behaviors and new thinking patterns are also needed to facilitate new, lasting, neural connections. (Don't worry, we'll get into all of that shortly!) Ketamine is simply the jumpstart that puts your brain back in a state of more effortless learning, like that of a child.

Another way you might think of ketamine is as a set of extremely powerful rocket boosters. No matter your starting point, making ketamine-assisted therapy part of your mental health game plan will give you a massive head start as you advance toward the destination of feeling more pleasant than unpleasant, more of the time, no matter what your goals.

A quick note about terminology: In this book, whenever I say "experience," I'm referring to a single dose. I'm talking about the time frame from the point when you first ingested the ketamine up to the point where you feel like it's out of your system.

"EXPERIENCE" CAN ALSO ENCOMPASS YOUR PREPARATIONS AND PLANNING. EARLY ON, AS I BEGAN HAVING PSYCHEDELIC EXPERIENCES, ONE OF MY GUIDES SAID THAT THE MOMENT YOU SET THE TIME THAT YOU'RE GOING TO TAKE THE MEDICINE IS, IN FACT, THE TRUE BEGINNING OF THE EXPERIENCE.

Some people in the ketamine community lump various terms together, using "trip," "journey," and "experience" interchangeably. I don't fully agree with that, because "trip" feels so much more loose, more party-ish, and less therapeutic. For our purposes, your "ketamine journey" will refer to the whole time you are in ketamine-assisted therapy, while your "ketamine experience" will be each individual session with the molecule.

How does ketamine work in the body and brain?

Apologies in advance for this hefty dose of jargon! Ketamine works primarily on the NMDA receptors in your brain, receptors which handle tasks including learning and memory. (NMDA stands for N-methyl D-aspartate, but you don't need to worry about that for our purposes.)[1] As you may know, your brain has chemical messengers, called neurotransmitters. These messengers work by binding to receptors on neurons (brain cells) to regulate brain activity. Receptors are the component of a neuron responsible for absorbing or releasing chemicals.

The primary way ketamine works is by blocking NMDA receptors on a particular type of neuron. Those neurons act like a gas pedal, making another type of neuron "put the brakes" on parts of the brain that usually release the neurotransmitter glutamate. This process is called "disinhibition," and is the way ketamine indirectly creates a "glutamate surge."

"Your brain on ketamine" looks like a brain with extra glutamate floating around. This abundance of glutamate stimulates, or excites, the brain—putting your brain in a more neuroplastic state than normal.

Neuroplasticity—aka neural plasticity or brain plasticity— describes your brain's ability to create new connections, aka, learn.

Basically, increased neuroplasticity = increased capacity to change our lives for the better.

In addition to its action at the NMDA receptors, ketamine is also known to work on many other types of receptors in the brain. Ketamine's effect on these processes are not as well researched as the action at the NMDA receptor site, but what is known, generally, is that they are part of ketamine's action in clearing cortisol in the brain and reducing overall pain and inflammation in the body. These other receptors may also be more involved in the antidepressant effect of ketamine than is the action at the NMDA receptor sites.

The long-story-short about how ketamine works can be found in the fact that ketamine is what's known as a "dirty drug." Which, contrary to what you might expect, isn't bad. It simply means that, as mentioned above, the molecule binds to many different targets in the brain and body, and therefore has a wide range of effects. This means that isolating specific effects of the drug is very hard to do for research, since research requires isolation of factors to be considered legitimate. But it also means that in practical use, ketamine looks like a wonder drug that helps unravel many different symptoms and creates the neural plasticity required for lasting relief.

Too good to be true? Perhaps, if not for understanding the broad range of actions ketamine has on whole brain processes. These whole brain processes make decisions about the management of every system in the body and run what can be considered the body's energy budget. (You'll learn more about that later.)

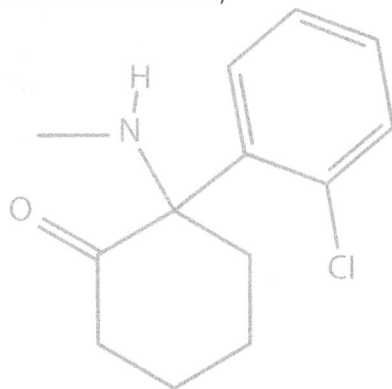

What does the ketamine experience feel like?

1 A non-ordinary state of consciousness

That might sound like a huge deal. Actually, though, a non-ordinary state of consciousness is occurring any time you are out of what you perceive to be your regular state of perceiving the world.

A non-ordinary state of consciousness can be as tiny as spinning around in circles before suddenly stopping. Or you can find a non-ordinary state of consciousness in the deepest depths of the mystical—or anywhere in between.

2 The movie of your life

You could compare the hallucinations induced by ketamine to reading a truthful, detached account of your life. You may see things—memories included—in your visuals at the time of your experience, in the same way that reading great fiction can put you in an immersive mental state.

For some people, it'll be more like being able to see the other person's side of a traumatic experience. With the sting taken out of the encounter, you can see different sides of the story, which rounds out your understanding of what happened—and what that experience will mean for you, going forward.

Not that the person who hurt you is right and you're wrong! More like: you finally understand what motivated them to pull the sh*t that really messed you up. You still might not be very happy with how things went down, but you'll see a new perspective of what was going on.

3 None of this is real — but that's not the point

If you find it helpful, you can remind yourself that what you're seeing isn't real—in case it seems scary or overwhelming.

Alternatively, you could use the experience as an opportunity to notice the words you're using to describe your experience, and therefore, how you're actively constructing your reality in the moment. This practice will facilitate and enhance the natural mind-revealing point of the whole experience. For example, say you find yourself describing the novelty of a ketamine experience as scary, overwhelming, or bizarre. In that moment, you actually have an opportunity to channel your focus toward a gentle curiosity about how you're constructing that reality, instead of being uncontrollably swept up in the judgment that it's "scary."

What is "real" in that moment is that you're safe, because you prepared and you have a sitter standing by if needed. (Right?!) Your task, then, is to simply notice the details of your reactions to the experience rather than believing them to be what is "real." What meaning am I assigning to the sensory experience I am having? What words am I using to name this experience of losing control? These chaotic perceptions? This loss of my normal frame of reference?

4 Expect the unexpected – and the familiar

As you're in the experience, you can expect what you've been thinking about in the previous week or so to reveal itself in what you're seeing or thinking. Expect to lose control of the direction of your thoughts. It's a bit of a paradox, because we do tell you to have an intention—but then you can't control where you're going.

If that seems counterintuitive, remember that none of this is linear. What that means for those of you (myself included!) who are used to setting goals that you proceed toward in a linear fashion... Don't go into your experience with that kind of plan in place.

In fact, your intention should be to stay mostly separate from your expectations. As I'll explain in the next chapter, your intention can be as simple as being open to what comes, with an overarching hope that things will get better.

Let's say your intention is to let go of emotional pain within you. You don't have to know what that will look like to understand that, in ketamine's nonlinear fashion, you're highly likely to wind up reaching your goal.

Overall, expect your ketamine experience to be very nonlinear. That said, think of intention more as an anchor and not a map. If you find yourself caught in a mental loop that you want to exit, use the anchor of your intention to pull yourself back in the direction you want to head.

YOUR INTENTION IS YOUR
ANCHOR

Is Ketamine a new drug?

NOT AT ALL. In 1962, ketamine was first synthesized and named (for its dual components of a "ketone" plus an "amine") by a professor of organic chemistry named Calvin Stevens, Ph.D.[2] For decades now, ketamine has been a go-to anesthesia medicine for dentists who need to sedate patients, even very young kids and the elderly. Emergency rooms use ketamine all the time for patients with gunshot wounds. Every single day, around the world, ketamine is used for anesthesia at 10 times the "mental health dose" (i.e. the doses you'd be taking in ketamine-assisted therapy).[3]

Is Ketamine-Assisted Therapy new?

Nope! Ketamine has been used therapeutically (but technically off-label) since some time shortly after it was first introduced as an everyday anesthetic. Like the "classical" psychedelics LSD and magic mushrooms, ketamine was swept up in the short-lived psychedelic revolution of the 1960s and 1970s.[4]

(So-called classical psychedelics like LSD, psilocybin, mescaline, and DMT work on the serotonin receptors in the brain. This is opposed to ketamine, which works largely on the glutamate receptors and therefore is considered to be a non-traditional psychedelic.)

Used to achieve striking (but sometimes controversial) results in treating various mental health conditions, ketamine then fell out of favor as a valid treatment method in the midst of the 1980s and 1990s' infamous War on Drugs.

A British psychiatrist named Humphry Osmond, M.R.C.S. is credited with coining the term "psychedelic" in the 1950s. The roots of this word, from Greek, boil down to an essential meaning of "mind revealing." Previous terms for this class of medicine (just two examples being "schizomimetic" and "psychotogenic") had been clunky and full of bad connotations.

The switch to the term "psychedelic" marked a positive sea change in how researchers were thinking about these medicines. That is, the psychedelic revolution marked a move away from a focus on hallucinations—the user's visual/auditory perception of things that do not exist to other people—and towards an understanding that **THESE DRUGS SIMPLY ILLUMINATE OR REVEAL WHAT WAS IN THE MIND ALL ALONG.**

PSYCHEDELIC MEANS

mind revealing

Are we sure that ketamine is safe?
Will I *feel* safe during my ketamine experiences?

YES. From a standpoint of objective, physical safety, there is so much data on ketamine proving that it's totally safe. After all, it's used every day in hospitals and doctor's offices worldwide. Out of 40,000 doses administered by a home dosing program that I work with, up to this point there have been zero medical emergencies. In addition, as you begin your ketamine journey, your prescriber will screen you for contraindications, so you can rest assured that they will be keeping your safety top of mind.

Then there's the question about your subjective experience of safety (or the lack thereof). No mental health professional wants to put someone in a traumatic experience—or even a trancelike state—that doesn't feel safe. Going in, it might help to remember that ketamine's anesthetic powers will act to dial down your physiological awareness. This means that subjectively, you are very unlikely to feel overwhelmed or panicked, like you might on a traditional psychedelic. Ketamine is gentler.

THE MOST IMPORTANT THING TO REMEMBER is that ketamine preserves respiratory function. So even if you're totally out of it, or you think terrible things are happening, or you feel like your heart isn't beating at all, or you feel like your heart is beating way too fast, hold on to the truth that your respiratory function is perfectly preserved. Even if you're thinking things are irrevocably out of whack, you have your sitter to make sure that things are very much not out of whack, and to assure you of that fact.

SAFE

Ketamine preserves respiratory function.
Your healthcare provider screens for contraindications.

Why ketamine for mental-health treatment (instead of another psychedelic)?

1. Ketamine is legal

The number-one reason to choose ketamine is a practical one: Ketamine is legal for medical use across the United States. Like most, if not all, legal medications in the United States, ketamine's FDA approval for one purpose (i.e. anesthesia) doesn't keep it from being used off-label, for other purposes—like the kind of personal transformation you might be hoping for.

2. Ketamine is gentler

The second reason to choose ketamine over the classical psychedelics is more about the quality of your experience. Ketamine is, in many ways, "easier" than other psychedelics because it's an anesthetic.

Think about what's going on in our bodies in REM (rapid eye movement) sleep, the phase of sleep when much of our dreaming occurs. During REM, the body is technically mildly paralyzed. That lack of movement actually limits the sensory data entering the brain. As you know, what we dream about usually has nothing to do with the actual setting where we're sleeping. So where we really are and how we're really feeling at that moment doesn't affect the visuals that make up our dreams.

Ketamine, like REM sleep, has an anesthetic nature. This literally means that ketamine produces partial or total loss of sensation. Ketamine's anesthetic nature limits (and distorts) the sensory information reaching your brain. For most people, this adds up to a first deep psychedelic experience that feels gentler, and not so overwhelming as they might have feared.

chapter

2

Who Stands to Benefit from Ketamine-Assisted Therapy?

Ketamine-assisted therapy is for

anyone who's curious about how they can grow as a person and feel happier every damn day—I'm talking therapy curious, ketamine curious, psychedelic curious.

anyone who's experienced trauma. And I don't mean just a single traumatic event. I also mean anyone who's really wrapped up in problematic patterns of dealing with the world, or noxious relationships that haven't served their needs.

Ketamine is an effective treatment ally whether you've experienced little-t trauma (interpersonal conflict, infidelity, loss, long-term instability or uncertainty, legal trouble, financial worries, etc.), big-T Trauma (sexual assault, natural disaster, terrorist attack, combat experience, etc.), or CPTSD–complex post-traumatic stress disorder (deeply rooted maladaptive patterns of interpersonal relating and self-regulation that began in childhood).

IT'S IMPORTANT TO NOTE that anyone with complex post-traumatic stress probably won't find resolution with a one-off or a six-dose ketamine journey. That's going to require, at minimum, a two or three-year journey of intensive work with someone who knows your whole story. In every case, the journey can and should incorporate a practice or a program of learning new thought patterns and behaviors.

The following are some examples of people who have been helped by a ketamine journey.

A veteran who was not happy with his authoritarian parenting style: lots of spankings, just generally very aggressive with and around his children.

A business owner. His business was doing well, and his intimate relationships were good enough, but he'd get to a point beyond which he could not go any further emotionally. He'd just shut down and turn off any chance at connection. An ongoing thought for him was, "Is this all there is to life?"

A white-collar professional who lost a child and could not seem to come out of the resulting intractable depression and hopelessness. At about 10 doses (with integration), he finally lifted up out of that pit, and was able to smile and authentically joke around. Back at about six doses, he was still worried he'd never get his life back.

These are just a few of the people I have personally worked with for whom a ketamine journey has been nothing short of life-changing.

In addition to the red-alert problem-solving nature of ketamine-assisted therapy, it is also an especially useful option for those of you who've tried therapy in the past but haven't gotten the results you wanted, for whatever reason. I'm thinking of one woman I work with who, like many of her fellow millennials, has dipped in and out of therapy over the last decade in search of solutions for her chronic, low-grade anxiety and depression.

She says that pre-ketamine, she would have described her time in therapy as unsatisfying, inefficient, and ultimately pointless. Just two ketamine journeys and two integration sessions later, she has immediately actionable insights and greater levels of self-confidence than she's felt since childhood.

> IF YOU DON'T CONSIDER YOURSELF TO BE "THE THERAPY TYPE"...
> IF YOU'VE BEEN BURNED BY A BAD PAST EXPERIENCE WITH THERAPY...
> IF YOU'RE NOT SURE THAT THERAPY WILL WORK IN THE WAY YOU NEED IT TO...
> Consider ketamine-assisted therapy.

Ketamine is supposed to work well on treatment-resistant depression, right?

CORRECT. If you've heard anything about ketamine in the news recently, it was probably in connection with the startling results the scientific community keeps seeing regarding adults battling treatment-resistant depression. In September 2022, a new study made headlines for proving ketamine's effectiveness in reducing suicidal thoughts, depression, and anxiety in over 400 adults over a year-long period.[1] Roughly 75% of these patients saw their moods improve. Even more striking, almost 40% of participants claimed to be symptom-free after 10 ketamine infusions. (For context, 19 to 34% of depressed adults feel absolutely no symptom relief, even after at least six weeks of standard-dose antidepressants.)[2]

treatment-resistant
DEPRESSION

A simple way to understand how ketamine creates these outcomes is to know that the way ketamine works, in large part, is by putting us back in the brain state of a child—in a good way! As adults, we have to actively apply ourselves if we want to learn new concepts and implement new behaviors. If you've ever started studying a new foreign language as an adult, you know what I'm talking about. It's really hard, right? Kids, by contrast, easily pick up new words and dialects—seemingly without having to try.

You probably know that one of the hallmark symptoms of depression is an overwhelming lack of energy. If you're depressed, you don't have any energy to spare because your body's energy budget[3] has been severely depleted for too long. From that starting point, how are you supposed to gather the wherewithal to actually start on all the behaviors that would make you feel better? With ketamine on board, that daunting prospect suddenly becomes a lot more realistic.

What about anxiety disorders? Will ketamine help with my OCD?

AS A MATTER OF FACT, YES. There are loads of anecdotes about ketamine's value in helping people with anxiety.

My client Joey, for example, was relatively debilitated by his habit of catastrophic thinking about the future, aka worrying, and by negative self-talk that made his brain continually send his body into high-alert energy production mode. This energy mode is perfect for big-time problem-solving and learning or for massive physical exertion, but not so great for everyday functioning in predictable environments. As a result, he was too charged up most of the time to focus productively or enjoy the good things about his life. He was at least mildly irritable most of the time, he felt like he always had to drink or use cannabis to take the edge off his agitation, and his behavior generally made him come across as someone who didn't care about other people.

Six doses of ketamine and a methodical program of integration over a three-month period helped his brain shift his body's energy budget out of overdrive and into a normal speed. His days felt more pleasant overall. His worrying and negative self-talk only dialed up on an occasional basis. He noticed that his need to reach for the sedating effects of alcohol and cannabis diminished dramatically—so much so that at a certain point he simply stopped remembering to bring his cannabis vape pen with him in the mornings. He also noted that his girlfriend commented that she felt like he cared more about her.

Now, about true obsessive-compulsive disorder (OCD). From the perspective of simple energy function, OCD is nothing more than one of the most dramatic and debilitating forms of a high-alert, high-energy state. A person makes sense of their high-alert, high-energy state with an obsessive thought (someone might break in) that they believe their compulsive action (I have to check the lock) will alleviate. When the compulsive action doesn't have the desired effect, they loop from thought to action to thought to action endlessly in an attempt to soothe their high-alert, high-energy state. Talk about being stuck!

Some people joke and describe their generally functional "obsessions" as OCD. But anyone diagnosed with OCD knows it is no joke, and far from a functional state of being. Unfortunately, there isn't much scientific literature about the value of ketamine for OCD. That is, however, less about ketamine's effectiveness and more about the fact that there have been very few clinical trials to date demonstrating the value of ketamine for OCD. As ketamine is increasingly proven effective on other mental health disorders, there has been an accompanying upsurge in studies applying ketamine to OCD. So far, the results of these studies are very promising.[4]

Should you proceed with ketamine if you're using (or maybe even abusing) other substances on a regular basis?

Potentially, yes.[5] In fact, ketamine can be a pathway to letting go of gray-area drinking or other unhealthy habit loops.[6] (Ketamine has recently shown very promising results in the treatment of eating disorders.)[7] One of ketamine's potential effects is a significant drop in cravings for alcohol, food, and other addictive behaviors/substances.

drug addiction food **addictive** sex
BEHAVIORS binge
work alcoholism

Let's say you suspect that you're drinking (or overeating, or smoking, or engaging in any other counterproductive pattern) to take the edge off other mental health symptoms. Ketamine-assisted therapy will first help you figure out why you feel like you need these other substances. Then, ketamine will eventually help you get to a place where you don't feel the urge towards your addiction so strongly or so often.

WITH KETAMINE-ASSISTED THERAPY, YOU CAN FINALLY STOP NUMBING OUT AND INSTEAD START FIGURING IT OUT.

Can ketamine help you better understand present and past relationships?

VERY. MUCH. SO. I can even give you a personal example. My mother can be really intense. A few of my most vivid childhood memories center on seeing my mom's "angry eyes" after I'd behaved badly or made some mistake.

In one of my very first ketamine experiences, I saw my mother's eyes completely differently. What I'd always thought of as "angry eyes," I suddenly saw as frightened. The life-changing insight was that her eyes were less about me being "bad" and more about the concern she felt for my safety and my future.

I happened to be videotaping myself during that ketamine experience, so I have on record the exact moment where it dawned on me and I said out loud, "OH." In the two years since, my understanding of my mother and our shared history has dramatically broadened. I no longer see that illusion of intense rage in her actions or facial expressions. This is just one personal example of how ketamine allows our brains to synthesize new thoughts into past experiences, allowing us to understand people and their actions in a new, more constructive way.

It's important to note that at this point in my therapy journey I'm not sure I would have ever reached this insight without ketamine. Realistically, I don't see myself as landing on that realization through the lens of normal conscious awareness. Those memories just don't affect my daily life in a drastic enough way that I would have been motivated to dig in of my own accord.

But that's one of the great things about this medicine: **IT BRINGS TO US WHAT WE NEED TO SEE SO THAT WE CAN MOVE FORWARD TOWARD OUR LIFE GOALS.** If you think that sounds a little too fantastical, refer to the examples of the experiences of the real people in this book. The consistencies in effects on diverse people are just too astonishing to discount.

I would consider myself a spiritual or religious person.
How will ketamine interact with my existing worldview?

Hang in there with me for a sec as I take a roundabout way to answer this question. I want to make it concrete for you, so I have to explain some body and brain stuff first.

To exist in and perceive this world as a human, you have a body. That body can be aroused or fatigued. And I don't mean sexual arousal. In physiological terms, aroused means energized. So, as I was saying, we call that spectrum of arousal or fatigue many different things. We can be activated or idle, and for our purposes I'm simply calling those states high energy and low energy.

Check out this mood graph

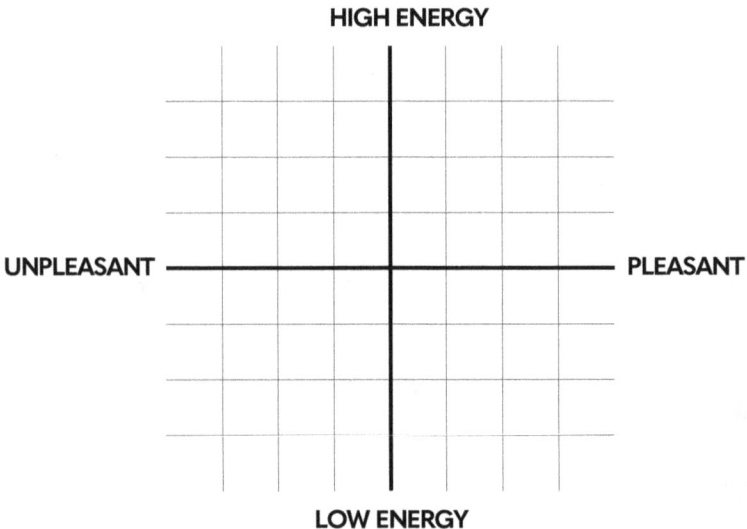

HIGH ENERGY

UNPLEASANT ————————————— PLEASANT

LOW ENERGY

On the vertical axis is "arousal." Up is high energy, down is low energy. On the horizontal axis, we have pleasantness and unpleasantness—what psychologists will often call "valence." In every moment of our lives, all of us will find ourselves somewhere in these quadrants. Your location on the graph depends on what's going on both internally and externally at that moment, which we colloquially call "mood." (Neuroscientists and psychologists call it "core affect.")

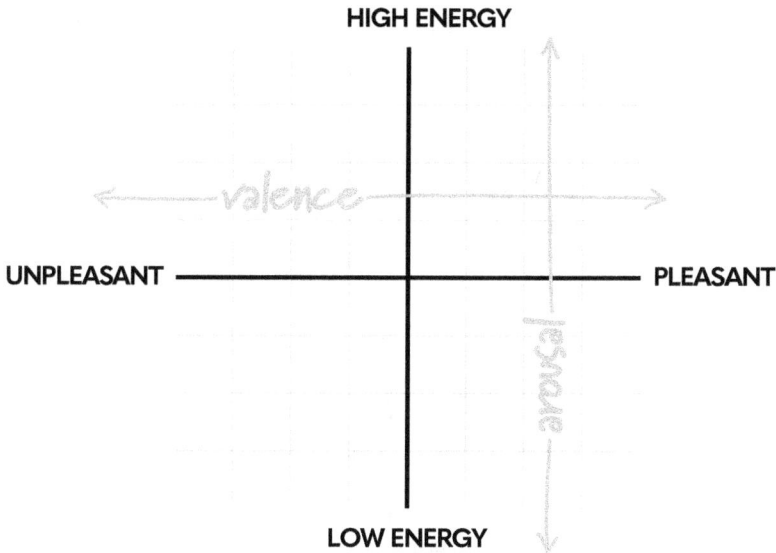

HIGH ENERGY

valence

UNPLEASANT ——————————————————— PLEASANT

arousal

LOW ENERGY

Valence + Arousal = Mood (aka Core Affect)

In addition, at all times, your body has an energy budget that your brain is managing. As humans, we're always spending, saving, or building energy. Your internal state and your external context both contribute to (and withdraw from) that energy budget. Note that sometimes I may just refer to this as your "body budget."[8]

your body's energy budget

A lot of times you're right in the middle of that graph, where you feel…fine. You don't have a whole lot (or any real lack) of energy. Things are neither super pleasant nor super unpleasant. If, however, you're somewhere way out on the edges, where the affect feels more intense, you're much more likely to identify it as an emotion, depending on context.

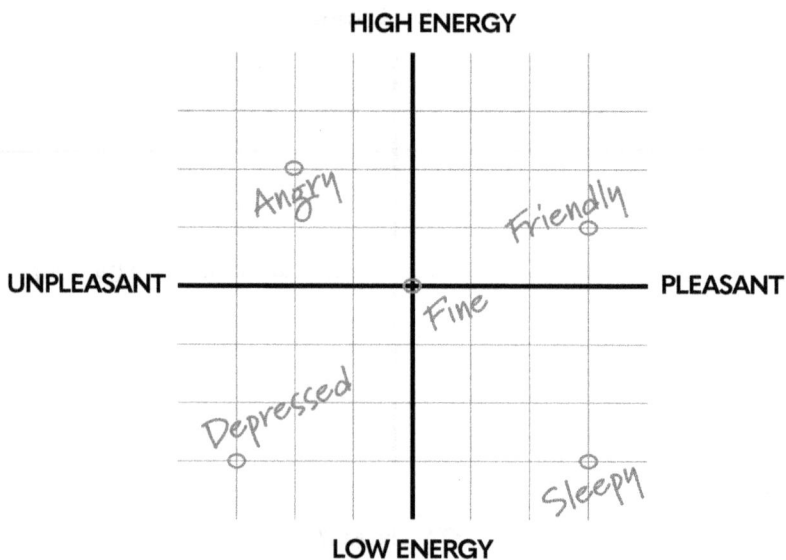

HIGH ENERGY

Angry

Friendly

UNPLEASANT ————————————⊕———————— PLEASANT

Fine

Depressed

Sleepy

LOW ENERGY

This is a mood graph with charted emotions

Whether you're in the center of the graph and feeling "fine" or you're out at the edges and calling the mood something specific, like excitement, depression, agony, or ecstasy, there are five levers you can pull to adjust where you are in the quadrants.

5 FIVE LEVERS

1. **Food/supplements/vitamins/fluids** *anything put into or on the body —even sunlight*

2. **Sleep/meditative restoration**

3. **Movement/breathing exercises/music**

4. **Communities/relationships**

5. **Concepts/ideas/mindset**

NOW, BACK TO RELIGION! World religions, and spiritual traditions, broadly speaking, are made up of concepts and ideas. (They are communities too, but right now we're focusing on concepts; Lever #5 of the Five Levers.) As far as science knows, humans are uniquely evolved to use concepts in order to regulate our body's energy budgets, and consequently our mood. So, far from being woo-woo, the concepts found in spiritual traditions and religion—like all concepts—regulate and alter our mood.

What happens then, is that under the influence of ketamine you're clearing cortisol from the brain,[9] you're fighting inflammation, you're modulating the immune system, and you're altering the function of some of the receptors in your brain. The right chemical soup is sloshing around in your skull so you can more easily fine-tune the concepts you're using to regulate your mood. Ketamine does this no matter what philosophical or religious viewpoint you bring to the table. In other words, ketamine works in conjunction with any religious or spiritual traditions that have previously served you or currently serve you.

First comes the new idea, then comes the new knowledge, then comes the new behavior, then comes the new mood. It doesn't matter where you got the ideas you're using to navigate life—philosophy, religion, or something your therapist said in last week's session—ketamine effectively greases the hinge behind the "concepts" lever so you can pull it all the more easily.

To paint the picture, I'll share Estrella's story.

Estrella is a professional with a successful, consistent 30-year work history. When she came to me, she was severely depressed, to the point that her weight was getting out of control and her grooming had begun to suffer. She had tried medications and other therapies with no success. She had no energy, felt terrible about herself, and was completely overwhelmed by the state of her family relationships. To manage, she journaled a bit, had some support from friends, and relied on concepts from Christianity, previous therapies, and various mindset mentors she studied. For a year, Estrella made excellent progress. She gained insights, rehearsed new ways of thinking about herself and her history, and practiced body-based therapy techniques to help her face stressful situations in a new way. She was on a positive trajectory, but would fall into low periods characterized by a return to self-hatred and old, dysfunctional stress-management practices. She would become frustrated by the ebb and flow of her progress, thinking at those times that she'd gone right back to where she started. There was no perspective available to Estrella showing the greater arc of her progress.

Being one of those people who holds on and tries to control things when she feels stressed, Estrella, like most people I work with, was skeptical about the idea of ketamine therapy. In spite of that skepticism, she took some time to educate herself and ultimately decided that the unknown was worth a try if it meant she'd speed her progress.

For Estrella, the once or twice per week frequency of ketamine experiences as suggested by the prescriber was impossible. She had long gaps between her experiences during most of her journey— sometimes as long as two months. Regardless, Estrella consistently made her way through the getting-to-know-you phase with ketamine. She began to notice quantitative shifts in her thinking and behaviors, and to feel a qualitative shift in her mood.

She also began to have an easier time applying the concepts from her Bible study classes to her life in concrete ways. She found herself consuming and applying many new ways of understanding herself and her life circumstances.

Her family relationships improved, she got her body's energy budget under control, began relating differently in stressful work situations, and noticed a decrease in her habit of feeling like a bad person who was at fault in all relationship situations.

A MAJOR BREAKTHROUGH came for Estrella after an unexpected mystical/ dissociative experience occurred. During that particular ketamine experience, the circumstances at the time created a mindset that brought Estrella back to one of the scariest moments of her life. It was a memory from when she was two years old. During that experience, Estrella relived a situation that, for nearly her entire life, had been fueling negative fundamental beliefs about her value as a human being. It was a difficult and confusing session, and required a couple weeks of deep reflection before she felt she'd emerged from its impact. But going forward, the insights and internal shifts of self-concept began to come even more rapidly.

She developed the ability to see her life and progress from a "meta" perspective that she'd never had. Being tired, unhappy, or cranky didn't mean she was back to square one. She could feel authentically angry, overwhelmed, or otherwise unpleasant—and simultaneously be completely aware that it was fine to be feeling that way, knowing that the horrible feeling would pass. It was as if she was an observer of herself while also being the participant. She began looking forward to donning the protective cloak of ketamine so she could explore hitherto impossible emotional states.

The cumulative effects of a slow, steady progression toward mental health goals and life intentions—followed by an avalanche of change after a mystical, somewhat unpleasant experience—are not uncommon. They form a pattern that has occurred for many of the people I've worked with on ketamine journeys.

First of all, know that you don't have to be at all open to mystical experiences for ketamine to work on you. That's because ketamine's safety and effectiveness is fully backed by scientific research.

WOO-WOO?

That said, it's totally understandable to feel nervous or uncomfortable before your first dose. You're entering an altered state of consciousness, after all. And maybe you don't see yourself as someone who does drugs—ever. I myself was super chicken about dipping my toes into the ocean of psychedelic experiences. I'm a bit of a goody-two-shoes, a control freak, whatever you want to call it.

But I made it through those first ketamine journeys, slowly but surely dialing my doses all the way to the top edge of mental health dosing. With patience and an open mind, getting to that mystical place has felt nothing but completely safe.

You might be asking yourself, *but does that mystical place get sh*t done, really?* Actually, yes. Just not necessarily in the linear way that control freaks are used to. **IN FACT, 90% OF THE PEOPLE I'VE WORKED WITH FEEL THAT THEIR JOURNEY WAS VALUABLE ENOUGH THAT THEY WOULD DO IT AGAIN IF NECESSARY OR PROACTIVELY BENEFICIAL TO THEIR LIFE GOALS.** I have a client, Kyla, who was initially very ketamine skeptical. She said, "When you take ketamine, it's like it tells you, "This is the level you should be on and opens the door for you to do the life-changing practices you know you should be doing." Long story short, you don't have to believe in "magic" for the magic to (safely) happen to you.

the basic pulse of life

E X P A N S I O N contraction

NOW, SPIRITUALITY. Let me make it concrete so you see how the "mystical" part of the experience might actually benefit you. First, I want you to think about "spirit" simply as unconfined energy. It's not contracted into matter. It's not directed in any particular way. It's expansive. Therefore, to experience "spirituality," if you're not a "spiritual" person, you'll simply have to find yourself in a more expansive physical state. A less physically contracted, less focused, state. Under the influence of ketamine, your body will be free of the typical contractions it holds so you can get things done (remember, it's an anesthetic), and you'll be experiencing the world through a non-ordinary (for you) lens. In summary, spirituality can be experienced in the body, whether you consider that "spirituality" or not.

What falls under the categories of expansion and contraction?

	EXPANSION	CONTRACTION
PHYSICAL	Breathe In Heartbeat; blood comes in Parasympathetic	Breathe Out Heartbeat; blood goes out Sympathetic
MOVEMENT	Rest	Action
MENTAL	Brainstorming Problem Solving Lantern Focus	Get Things Done Applying Solutions Flashlight Focus
THINGS YOU INGEST	Ketamine	Coffee

Two basic categories that simplify a lot of stuff.

Another way to think about it is: The body is contracted energy. It's matter. Spirit is expansive energy. It's unbounded energy. In life, we're always going back and forth between contraction and expansion. When I'm contracted, I'm making things happen. I'm blocking out other stuff to get things done. I'm focused.

When I'm expansive, I'm open to awareness of a wider range of data. I'm soft. I'm open. The rule maker in my brain is taking a rest. I'm capable of brainstorming, capable of seeing things from another person's point of view, etc. Some people will call that state "spirituality." Rest assured, there are very specific things happening in the brain that make this happen, but for now we'll leave it at that.

In conclusion, to all my hardcore atheists out there: Be patient with yourself, and don't worry about accomplishing anything at first other than just getting yourself used to the experience. Like anything else in life, it's not until you do something a bunch of times that you're an expert. The more ketamine experiences you have, the deeper you can explore, and the richer the value you'll get out of it—whether or not you identify as a spiritually-inclined person.

Can ketamine help someone going through a breakup?

ABSOLUTELY. In large part, the anguish of a breakup is based on the interruption of simple energetic and chemical functions in the body. Someone who's been recently dumped would probably feel lots better if she ate a wholesome diet, stopped drinking away her sadness, and started a workout routine that resonates with her abilities and proclivities.

But these levers—food and movement—are levers that she can't pull right now because she just doesn't have the energy. When we have invested in someone and they decide to leave us, their sudden absence in our life can wreak havoc on our body's energy budget. In the case of a breakup, community is the highly relevant lever. When they leave, we lose whatever regular contribution they were making to our body's energy budget.

So we're learning to live without them (aka: encoding a prediction error), which we perceive as highly unpleasant (aka: negative affect/mood). Translation: Our brains continue to expect good/happy stimulation and energy input that is suddenly unavailable.

Complicating matters, learning requires the presence of certain chemicals in our bodies (namely, acetylcholine and norepinephrine) that can feel unpleasant if, for whatever reason, we don't want to be doing said learning. It is a massive "learning" task to process the fact that your ex is no longer there to support your body's energy budget.

Not to mention that crying and sadness are fatiguing in their own right! If you're going through a difficult breakup, maybe the most practical thing you can do is acknowledge that your body's energy budget is totally bankrupt and go from there.

What are simple ways that you can support your body in feeling more pleasant, even though this extremely unpleasant thing has happened and you're left to manage your body's energy budget all on your own? If exercising feels daunting and putting the wine down is a no-go, what can you do? You can do breathing exercises that charge your body up. You can take a five-minute walk. You can take a cold shower or plunge. These tiny actions will put tiny positive deposits in your body's energy budget.

Ketamine-assisted therapy would be a more significant positive deposit in your body's energy budget. If time is the best healer of a broken heart, ketamine can skip the clock ahead so you'll feel less awful, sooner.

Will ketamine help me accept who I really am, flaws and all?

Ketamine definitely makes it easier to accept ourselves as flawed individuals who nevertheless deserve love. Let me explain how that works, exactly.

When we're reminded of some part of ourselves that we feel is unacceptable, say, being greedy (or substitute any personality characteristic you want), there's an emotional or energetic charge that flares up within us. This charge can send us into and keep us locked in a physical state of chronic low-grade fight-or-flight (aka: hyperarousal or chronic stress). To summarize way more information than would fit in this book, such chronic low-grade hyperarousal feels stressful and unpleasant, and mostly blocks us from further learning and growth. End point: you constantly feel crummy and get down on yourself.

The tricky thing is: that overarousal comes from some past experience(s) that you may not actually remember on a conscious level. If some event in the present reminds you that you're greedy, you come face-to-face with an aspect of yourself that you know you're not <u>supposed</u> to be. You lock right into judgments of yourself and spiral down the self-hatred slide. (This might sound familiar if you've ever heard of the "shadow self" or the unconscious.)

the unconscious

formed in your first 7 years of life

shadow self

underworld

the stuff you don't know about yourself

THIS IS WHERE KETAMINE SAVES THE DAY, because its anesthetic quality minimizes physiological arousal. With ketamine's help, you'll be able to acknowledge and accept that you're greedy sometimes. You'll even be able to think calmly about the story that caused you to learn you were "greedy" and dislike yourself for that greed in the first place. You'll also be able to understand the "why" of your greed in that past moment, retroactively removing the self-judgment.

Safely separated from the pain and shame that the lesson burned into you, you're free to see the situation clearly, integrate any useful feedback, and (finally!) move forward with your life.

THAT IS TRUE SELF-ACCEPTANCE: Conscious awareness of your behavior from a more objective perspective, without the discomfort that clouded your attempt at compassionate self-appraisal. Self-loving, self-awareness is what we're after. Ketamine helps get us there.

Wait, how can I have a truly objective perspective on myself?

It's actually easier than you think. I alluded to it earlier when I explained the body's energy budget. A truly objective perspective of yourself is based on how brains function and why they exist. According to the latest "best guess" of brain science, brains exist to manage the complex systems of big bodies that move.[10] Long story short, your brain works 24/7 to control that energy budget I mentioned.

Emotions you have, movements you make, and things you think are all outcomes of (and levers you can pull to influence) the way your brain manages your body's energy budget.

Before this gets too complicated, what's important for our purposes is: Understanding your life from this "simple energy function" perspective will free you from your chains of self-hatred. Ketamine, should you choose it, can facilitate your mastery of this perspective.

simple energy functions

chapter 3

What to Expect on your Ketamine Journey

LET'S KICK THINGS OFF BY BRIEFLY TALKING ABOUT "SET AND SETTING."

It's a phrase that's used all the time in psychedelic circles, so we'll only spend a tiny bit of time on it here.

MIND set AND
setting

"SET" IS LITERALLY THE MINDSET YOU BRING TO THE KETAMINE EXPERIENCE.

And that can be extremely broad...

- *What happened earlier in the day?*
- *What's been on your mind lately?*
- *What do you think about the whole ketamine process?*
- *What do you think about yourself?*
- *What do you think about your surroundings?*
- *What intention, if any, have you set?*
- *What is the state of your body's energy budget?*
  (Believe it or not, this deeply influences mindset.)

"SETTING" IS EVEN MORE LITERAL.

It mostly refers to information you're getting from your five senses:

- *What's the air temperature?*
- *Are you having the ketamine experience in your bedroom? In your backyard? In a natural setting?*
- *Who is your sitter? (How do you feel about your sitter? What's your relationship to them?)*
- *Are you wearing comfy clothes?*
- *Does your environment smell good or bad?*
- *Is your pet or child making noise in the next room?*

"Set and setting" has become a psychedelic cliché for good reason: If you embark on your experience with a positive mindset and in a soothing setting, you're likely to have a good one. If your mindset is negative and your setting unsettling, your experience is less likely to be pleasant.

SETTING AN INTENTION IS ONE OF THE BEST WAYS TO GIVE YOURSELF AN ANCHOR POINT IF THE JOURNEY ITSELF GETS DISORIENTING.

YOUR

INTENTION
IS YOUR **ANCHOR**

Here are some example intentions to get you started:

I am ready to change bad habits.

I will be kind to myself.

I enjoy my life more often.

I want to improve my relationships.

I am ready to heal.

I want to improve my listening skills.

I am free of pain.

I surrender to what is.

Whatever your intention, keep it brief, simple, and free of any "should" statements. (i.e. I have to get over my trauma, I need to love myself.)

HERE'S AN EXAMPLE. One of my clients thought that people were misunderstanding her a lot of the time, and it was causing her some bit of anguish. She began her ketamine journey with an intention to be understood. During one of her experiences, she came to the conclusion that she cannot control whether people understand her or not, but that she can pay attention to what others are saying so that she responds more precisely to what they have said. This led to an intention to listen to others more carefully, and to "improve her listening skills."

Do I really need to set a specific intention?

YES, HOWEVER: Not everyone will know what their intention is going into their first ketamine experience—and that's totally okay! If you don't have a particular intention in mind going in, just **TRY TO STAY OPEN**. Your intention might come to you while you're "under"—and seemingly out of the blue. This is an especially useful game plan if you're looking into ketamine because you feel stuck in some way.

In fact, staying open was my intention going into my first ketamine experience, because my goal was simply to understand what clients would be going through. At the time, there wasn't any sort of consistent unpleasantness in my life that I was trying to unravel and resolve.

That's not to say that "be open" can't be your intention even if you are going in with a consistent unpleasantness you're looking to resolve. In that case, your intention might look something like: "I'm going to see what happens, knowing that I will be circling back around in a nonlinear way to resolving that problem."

IF YOU'RE WILLING to see what happens—whatever happens—you'll discover surprising things that'll help you know yourself more deeply. As weird as this may sound, it's a little like becoming a sommelier. Sommeliers, of course, know their wine so well that with one whiff, they can tell you it was grown in southern France in soil with a high limestone content, during a particularly rainy year. In the same way, the deeper you dive into your psyche, the more refined and accurate your view of yourself and the better your understanding of your thoughts and actions. That expanded and detailed self-knowledge will empower you to make better choices in every area of your life. Win-win!

> YOUR INTENTION DOESN'T HAVE TO BE ANYTHING MORE GRANULAR THAN: "I'M GOING TO SEE WHAT HAPPENS, WITH THE OVERALL AWARENESS THAT THIS IS A THERAPEUTIC PROCESS I'M ENGAGING IN MINDFULLY."

When is a good time to have a ketamine experience?

Choosing a good time for each experience will be a key part of making set and setting work for you. You don't want to have your ketamine experience right after receiving bad news, during a particularly stressful week at work, or at other moments when your body and mind are out of whack. Basically, a bad day is not a particularly good day for ketamine.

That said... If you're having a lot of trouble finding the right time for your experience, also know that there is no perfect time. By all means, be methodical about avoiding alcohol and caffeine in the hours leading up to your date with ketamine. (Alcohol[1] and caffeine[2] reduce the effects of ketamine.) By all means, select a day when you have time to recover fully after your out-of-body experience is complete. For instance, you could start early in the day so you have time for reflection and relaxation afterward. It's up to you, but feel free to be creative with the timing.

Keep in mind—while there certainly are better and worse times—there's no truly optimal timing for your experiences. Don't put so much pressure on yourself. Progress is more important than perfection.

How do I choose my sitter?

The most important quality you'll need in a sitter is straightforward: **THEY UNDERSTAND THAT YOU'RE COMPLETELY SAFE THROUGHOUT YOUR TIME UNDER THE INFLUENCE.** Your sitter can be someone who knows you super-duper well, or someone you trust but don't know all that well.

Another thing: Try to avoid asking a highly anxious person to be your sitter. If they hover over you constantly, their anxiety will start to have a negative effect on you. You want a sitter who's responsive, calm, and understands the broad contours of what you'll be experiencing.

I live alone, and it'd be somewhat inconvenient to arrange for a sitter. Do I really need one?

I'll give you a great example of why the sitter is so important to your journey. I worked with someone who'd had five or six experiences with her sitter nearby. Let's call her Jen. As is the case for most sitters, Jen's sitter didn't have to do anything. They were there "just in case."

During her seventh session, Jen started to feel alone and afraid because she'd entered a very mystical, dreamlike experience. In that moment, when Jen was completely disconnected from reality, she called for her sitter—but there was no answer.

Because things had been so uneventful up to that point, Jen's sitter briefly left to go to the hardware store. He hadn't discussed it with her beforehand, because everything had been totally fine in Jen's six previous sessions.

So poor Jen found herself completely disoriented and without her sitter present to reassure her that all was well. This experience is sometimes referred to as being "in a k-hole," by those who use ketamine at lower doses as a party drug and unknowingly take too much without understanding the mystical space they could end up in. Despite knowing that a mystical experience was not only possible but probable during her mental health dose, Jen was not able to be present comfortably without reassurance.

Luckily, there's a happy ending. As we discussed this upsetting experience in an integration session afterwards, Jen remembered that she had an old, underlying fear of abandonment going back to one particular childhood experience. Over the years, Jen had gotten so good at blocking out this fear that she usually didn't think about it at all.

Our brains are always taking in sensory data, even if we're not conscious of it. Despite Jen's complete immersion in her ketamine experience, she heard the door open and then close. Jen's brain had registered that her sitter wasn't there for her.

As I mentioned, and as you'll often hear folks in psychedelic circles say, "psychedelic" means "mind revealing." What gets revealed is, of course, what was in the person's mind all along, patiently waiting to be addressed. Jen's moment of discomfort and fear opened up an opportunity to explore and work through an old wound that she didn't even know still needed to be resolved.

Before addressing the fear via integration, Jen decided she didn't want to try ketamine ever again. Once I explained what happened, and Jen saw that she had been safe all along, she found new determination to keep exploring with ketamine. Because of the time and energy spent on integration, Jen now feels fully equipped to tackle further experiences head-on.

A sitter is doubly important if, like me, you're someone who thrives on always being in control. Having that sitter allows (forces?) us to accept that it's okay to have someone taking care of us. For some of us, relinquishing that need for control is part of what we're working through with the help of the medicine. In each subsequent ketamine session, you'll increasingly trust that you don't have to do anything, that you can safely relax and let others take care of you.

THE SITTER PROVIDES ALL KINDS OF VALUE TO YOUR EXPERIENCE— ESPECIALLY IF YOU REALLY DON'T FEEL LIKE YOU NEED ONE.

1. Intravenous (doctor's office)
2. Intramuscular (doctor's office)
3. Nasal spray (doctor's office or at home)
4. Sublingual rapid dissolve tablets (at home)
5. Suppository (at home)

5 delivery methods
IV, IM, NASAL, SUBLINGUAL, SUPPOSITORY

There are five different delivery types—three more commonly used in the presence of a doctor, and two which can be used at home without direct supervision by a medical professional. In medical settings, ketamine has long been administered as a shot into the muscles, or intravenously (IV). Over 20 years ago (February 2000), there was even a landmark study based on IV dosing. This study played a huge role in proving the effectiveness of ketamine for off-label use.[3]

If you wind up going to a ketamine clinic, you can probably expect them to use an IV. That method requires a doctor and being hooked up to various machines for extra monitoring. This is out of an abundance of caution that, frankly, is appropriate whenever any drug is being given intravenously. IV ketamine in a doctor's office almost never comes with integration time. That's because at a doctor's office, they are not in the business of providing therapy or integration services.

In addition to the clinics that do IV, a few practitioners (like psychiatrists) use intramuscular delivery (IM). Though this doesn't require as much doctor time as IV, it isn't used all that often because people (understandably!) tend to freak out wherever needles are concerned. To be honest, though, IM is my favorite delivery method.

One of the most recently developed methods—as in over the last 10 to 20 years—is the rapid dissolve tablet (RDT) under the tongue.[4] This is called sublingual dosing, and is available via home-dosing ketamine clinics.

Another delivery method is a nasal spray delivery method. This can be done with generic ketamine or with Spravato®, a patented medication.[5] Keep in mind that if you opt for Spravato®, you'll have to go to a certified Spravato® treatment center approximately 12 times over eight weeks for a minimum of two hours per visit to have the medicine administered. (Not so with generic ketamine compounded for nasal administration.) Spravato®, though patented, has not been shown in research to be more effective than any other more time-honored delivery method of generic ketamine. One upside of the Spravato® nasal spray is that most insurances will cover it.[6] An important final note about nasal-spray delivery: It comes at a symptom management dosage rather than a dose that facilitates a "deep dive" and lasting change.

Lastly, there is the suppository delivery method. This is the most infrequently prescribed delivery method at the moment, so you might have a difficult time finding a prescriber who will dose with this delivery method.

The ketamine itself does not cost a lot of money. It's the time that you spend with your healthcare providers that drives up the costs of ketamine-assisted therapy. That's why an at-home program is so valuable, because it opens up access to this really amazing mental health intervention. Is home dosage a panacea? Of course not. But it allows you to spend less money on administering the ketamine and more money on integration and therapy, which is where the transformation really occurs.

DOSING

analytic dose

therapeutic dose

mystical dose

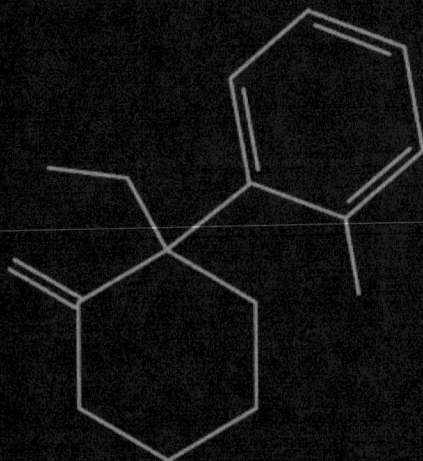

Dosing is important in just about every aspect of life: working out, drinking coffee or alcohol, maintaining a healthy weight, etc.

With the therapeutic use of ketamine, different doses can help you achieve different goals. The following are the 3 basic dosing levels for mental health. I've left out specific numbers in this chart because your prescriber will make decisions about specific dosages for you, depending on the delivery method, your goals, and their assessments about your prior psychedelic experience and physical status.

ANALYTIC / PSYCHOLYTIC DOSE At this low dose, you can sit up and engage in a conversation with your therapist. It's a comfortable, relaxing dose that can induce a state of empathy with yourself and others. It might feel very mildly trancelike. Sensory perceptions are only very mildly distorted.

THERAPEUTIC DOSE At this higher dose, you want to lie down and conversation is no longer desirable. Personal introspection is very strong and hallucinations may occur. Mostly, you remain aware of your physical location and are able to move carefully to the bathroom, if needed. Sensory perceptions are dramatically distorted.

MYSTICAL DOSE This is the highest therapeutic dose. You are lying down and completely in another world, unaware of both the room you're in and the sitter beside you. You're in a hallucinogenic state, whether your eyes are open or closed. External sensory perceptions are radically distorted, if not completely eliminated. It is after being in this state that you'll have the greatest ability to put all your life experiences together in new ways and realize what's most important for you. This is also the dose at which the most significant physical brain changes occur. If some of that sounds alarming, remember this: Your brain will be taking care of your physical body, exactly the way it does when you are sleeping deeply, so you don't have to worry.

A sample timeline of a ketamine experience

*assuming you're taking the medicine orally

UP TO A DAY BEFORE: Decide with your sitter when and where you'll have the experience.

24 HOURS BEFORE: Stop consuming alcohol or anything else your prescriber tells you to avoid.

THE MORNING OF YOUR EXPERIENCE DAY: Limit caffeine intake. Now is not the time for a venti triple-shot red-eye!

2-4 HOURS BEFORE: Start fasting, but keep hydrating. (Defer to your prescriber's guidelines).

30 MINUTES BEFORE: Take the anti-nausea medication your ketamine provider supplied you. (Defer to your prescriber's guidelines).

15 MINUTES BEFORE (optional): Do a guided meditation or breathing exercise to relax. Get your music ready.

GAME TIME: Place the medicine under your tongue and let it dissolve for 15 minutes, swishing occasionally, without swallowing. (This will allow you to absorb more of the medication.) Spend part of this 15 minutes using the restroom one last time.

15 MINUTES LATER: Swallow the remaining medication, lie down, and put on your eye mask. You'll probably be feeling some effects by this point.

30-45 MINUTES LATER: You're probably feeling the peak of your dose.

1½ HOURS LATER: You'll experience a second, smaller peak as the ketamine is processed through your liver.

2 HOURS LATER: You'll start feeling more normal, but go easy on yourself—you're not ready to perform all your regular functions yet. Rushing to do so can be very unpleasant, not to mention counterproductive. Don't worry if this takes longer; sometimes it just does. Bodies metabolize substances at different rates, and the same body will metabolize at different rates on different days.

24 HOURS LATER: You'll probably feel 100% back to your regular self. You're free to perform any and all normal functions again, including driving a car if that applies to you.

48 HOURS LATER: The chemical soup in your brain is returning to a more normal state, and the window of optimal neural plasticity is closing. Hopefully you've spent the last two days exposing yourself to new thinking and new behaviors, because those are the foundation of long-term change.

chapter 4

Travel Alert: Caveats and Contradictions

Let's begin by setting some realistic expectations, namely: Ketamine is very much not a magic pill.

(OK, OK, I know. I refer to the "magic of ketamine" sometimes, but it's not really magic.) Ketamine experiences will not change anything long-term if you take no further action to change your life. Your ketamine journey is merely the door that opens the possibility for self-awareness, which hopefully will be followed by self-transformation. Ketamine will absolutely help you get started on that path. Regardless, your happiness always remains solely your responsibility.

Here's a non-exhaustive list of what I hear all the time about people's ketamine journeys. If you find yourself thinking any of the following, rest assured that you're far from alone.

"Um, I ordered bliss with a side of relaxation! What the heck is this?"

"I think this batch of pills must be bad or something, cause I didn't feel a thing."

"Is this actually working?"

"Wow, that was the most amazing thing."

"Is this really safe? Because I thought I was going to die."

"I thought I was losing my mind."

"I saw rows and rows of snakes / gothic lace / shag-carpeted staircases—and that's all I kept seeing for five sessions!"

"Are we absolutely sure I took ketamine? Because that was terrible."

"It was a beautiful / blissful / relaxing / wholly wonderful feeling."

"Am I doing this right?"

The clichés with which I answer?
"Each experience is different. Expect the unexpected. Expect ketamine to be different every time."

Next, let's get into the various objections some folks have to the notion of ketamine-assisted therapy.

The hallucinations, the revisiting of past experiences, the physical side effects—it's all too much! How am I supposed to change my life if I'm feeling completely and utterly overwhelmed?

Ketamine experiences can absolutely be overwhelming and full of "noise"—if you're not being simultaneously guided through a group integration process or one-to-one work with a therapist. An overall sense of confusion and discomfort might arise, which could end up turning some people off from the value of psychedelics in general. Please remember that this can all be avoided through the support of a proper integration framework.

The other way people get overwhelmed and turned off by ketamine is through the sheer speed at which it works. Since self-awareness is the goal of all therapy, it's not different from traditional therapies that utilize slower pathways to self-awareness. Ketamine's speed makes it both wonderful and potentially frightening. I'm sure you can imagine an excitable therapist pushing a client too far, too fast, without proper preparation—not to mention how those unfortunate instances harm ketamine's outstanding therapeutic reputation.

KETAMINE CAN BE WONDERFUL. KETAMINE CAN BE OVERWHELMING. IT'S PARAMOUNT TO HAVE BOTH THE TOOLS TO DEAL WITH OVERWHELM AND THE KNOWLEDGE THAT YOU'RE SAFE.

Of note: The most uncomfortable potential physical side effect is nausea. Nausea doesn't happen for everyone, nor does it happen every time for those who experience it. According to the pharmacist I consulted, nausea usually shows up at the end of the experience, if at all. Generally, for people who don't get nauseated easily, it is unlikely to be a problem, even without anti-nausea medication. Your prescriber will send an anti-nausea medication along with your ketamine doses, just in case. I HATE nausea, so I used the medication with devotion at the beginning of my journey. Now, I prefer to avoid it for the following reasons. Some of the medications cause constipation, some cause lengthy drowsiness. During your consultations, your prescriber will discuss different anti-nausea options with you.

Isn't ketamine a party drug?

Yes, ketamine has been abused by people trying to get lit. But you know what? Glue isn't for sniffing, yet some people still sniff it. I think we can all agree that there are plenty of substances out there that can be used either for good or for ill. Enough said.

Is there such a thing as a k-hole?

Yes—but you don't need to worry too much about falling into one. Remember Jen from earlier? She found herself in a k-hole, i.e., a mystical experience.

mystical experience

What k-hole really means is that you find yourself totally disembodied, as if you're in a dream from which you cannot escape. This place is not something to be scared of. With ketamine for mental health, this is the goal at least some of the time. **GO INTO THE JOURNEY KNOWING THAT ALL IS WELL.** Even if things get uncomfortable, you'll always return knowing that you've remained in a safe setting and that any discomfort will pass. Just like a bad dream, after the journey is over, you'll know that it was just a dream. In fact, after the dust settles, you're more likely than not to start seeing positive benefits as a result of the mystical experience.

If you've heard k-hole horror stories from recreational users of ketamine, I'll put your mind at rest. Let's say your intention was to party, but you become so anesthetized by excessive ketamine that you're lying there in your thoughts, distorted sensory information coming at you fast, all without being able to easily move. Of course that's going to feel terrible! (Rest assured: There is no dose taken for mental health reasons that will anesthetize you to the point where you literally cannot move.)

Yes, the right dose of ketamine can and will put you in a dream state that you can't "get out of" until the medicine wears off. Technically, one name people give that dream state is a k-hole. But if you're prepared for that state, whether it feels blissful or uncomfortable, the experience will be a valuable one that moves you toward your mental health goals. Since you know that getting to this mystical, dreamlike place is the goal at least some of the time, you'll know that no matter what happened while you were there, you were safe. **REMEMBER, IT'S ALL ABOUT SET AND SETTING.**

Does what I saw while under the influence mean something concrete?

Often people will tell me that they saw something specific either through an entire experience, or consistently from one experience to the next. Much like you might after a particularly vivid and memorable dream, they wonder what it all means.

HALLUCINATIONS

No one really knows, but my suspicion about repeated visual hallucinations is that they are a visual representation of something going on inside the body or gut—basically, some sensory data that's coming into your brain strongly in one experience or repeatedly across different experiences. In other words, your internal state plus things you've seen in the "real world" are coming together to create these visuals.

That's because your brain uses concepts (remember concepts from earlier) to make sensory signals meaningful. In this case, it's creating visual concepts to represent the sense data from inside your body. You don't have to know what the visual concepts mean to begin understanding them by using your imagination and following your associations to figure out what they mean to you. A good therapist can help you get skilled at doing this.

You could also end up being one of the people who fall totally asleep and don't remember anything. It's unusual, but has happened to me once—at the same dosage where I previously had confusing, difficult, and wonderful experiences. There's a whole range of what can and will happen subjectively, even with the same person at the exact same dosage.

Ketamine-assisted therapy can be a little bit like dream analysis. What are your associations with the elements and people in those dreams? Dreams are "psychedelic" in that they are mind revealing. But not in a concrete way, since dreams typically reveal what's on your mind in an abstract way.

Don't feel pressure to make linear meaning out of what you are seeing—at all. Don't get too caught up in the visuals, they might not mean anything. (And that's more than okay!) In fact, if you don't have vibrant visuals, or any visuals at all, don't worry. Not everyone does.

Isn't ketamine potentially addictive, though?

Sure, you could argue that.[1] If someone is repeatedly returning to an activity that provides them some positive outcome, is that really addiction? If going to the movies is a reliable escape from your unhappy home life, then you might say that in some ways you're "addicted to" the local multiplex. But you can rest assured that ketamine doesn't create the physical dependence that has long been linked to true addiction.

Let's be clear: Caffeine and sugar are both more physically addictive than ketamine. Physiologically, addiction develops when the receptors in your brain get used to a certain amount of something. Eventually, it takes more of the substance to get the same effect that you are used to. This does not happen with ketamine—1 mg/kg (or 0.5 mg/kg or 1.5 mg/kg) will forever have approximately the same level of effect on you. The novelty will wear off and some might chase the novelty of higher and higher doses, but the physiological effects remain the same.

Will or can I have a bad experience (trip)?

I don't like to use the term "trip" in the context of psychedelics for mental health, but since the term "bad trip" is so common, I thought I would use it here to speak to the specific term.

The idea of having a bad experience or trip while under the influence of ketamine is a common fear for many of my patients who've had unpleasant cannabis experiences, such as anxiety or panic attacks. Great news, if that's you: Ketamine is nothing like cannabis.

KETAMINE
relaxes
THE BODY

Since ketamine relaxes your whole body while perfectly maintaining respiratory function, you will almost certainly have an overall pleasant experience, especially at analytic and therapeutic dosing levels, and even at mystical doses once they are familiar to you. One of my clients has described it as the most wonderful feeling in the world, and I don't disagree. In the unlikely event that you do feel distressed at any point, your sitter will be there to calm and reassure you.

So many of my clients are people who feel positively terrified by any loss of control. If you've ever felt like your life (or your family's life, or your partner's life) is hanging on by a thread because of your efforts and your control...Just know that you're not alone. I myself was definitely a member of that club.

But this is a crucial part of the therapy journey: Feeling confronted by your discomfort and your demons. This work isn't always comfortable. Of course, no work of true value ever is.

Some of you have likely had more than one terrible cannabis experience, and fear ketamine might be the same. I'll level with you: You might, for about half a second, feel like you're going to go to that place where cannabis takes you. But then—surprise!—you don't. It's a completely different operating system. No stress.

You might also have heard lore about "bad trips" that comes from misrepresentations of some people's experiences taking psychedelics recreationally. (Thank you, War on Drugs). This generally happens when someone is in a negative mindset or an unsatisfactory setting when they take a psychedelic, and/or they have taken a larger dose than they expected and don't have the support they need. It is generally accepted by the therapeutic community that psychedelic experiences are never "bad" when they are conducted mindfully in a safe setting. They might be difficult, but not bad.

As I've mentioned several times, the possibility of an experience being bad or difficult with ketamine is extremely rare due to the anesthetic nature of the medicine. Any difficulty during a ketamine experience will be purely mental (unless you get nauseated). It's the classical psychedelics, not ketamine, that generally come with a dose of physical overarousal and the label of "bad" when they get difficult.

Is there anyone who's not a good candidate for ketamine?

Out of an abundance of caution, yes. People with active psychosis, which may include visual or auditory hallucinations, should not embark on any ketamine journeys. This is standard across the world of ketamine-assisted therapy, largely because of liability issues. It's wise practice, generally speaking, to hold the line on serving psychedelics to patients who have been diagnosed with schizophrenia. That doesn't mean there isn't some research literature out there on the use of psychedelics for people suffering from schizophrenia, but the field isn't yet at a point where that's standard across the board.

There are also a few miscellaneous medical and physiological issues that will keep someone from safely pursuing ketamine. You as a client don't have to worry about that, though, because your prescriber will thoroughly screen you for any medication conflicts or contraindications. High blood pressure is the big one. It doesn't mean you don't qualify; it just means extra precautions will be put in place.

Will ketamine fundamentally change who I am?

As a therapist, I would say that we don't change. We simply add to who we are, and ketamine does facilitate that.

CHANGE **we add to who we are**

Before I go any further,
let's define change for our purposes in this book.

Wanting to change = Wanting to do / act / think differently in situations where we currently behave in ways that are not serving us / our goals / the people we care about.

The science of habit formation has proven that we can't ever fully eradicate old habits. Realistically speaking, the best we can do is to introduce and practice new habits to the point that they eventually override our old patterns. In conclusion, change is really more about adding flexibility to your choices than it is about removing the old choices that you used to habitually make.

Hate to say it, but your mom was right: People don't change. People simply supplement the range of actions and thoughts that they have in particular moments so those actions and thoughts can serve their goals better.

I heard that ketamine makes you dissociate, though... That sounds bad. Isn't dissociation bad?

Ketamine is dissociative because it's an anesthetic. Ketamine disconnects your conscious awareness from sensations in your body and allows you to reflect on past experiences without feeling any unpleasant high energy associated with those memories. Ketamine also allows (forces, perhaps) some people to experience "losing your mind," which is one way of describing what happens when you dissociate or disconnect from your body.

Let me back up for a second. A big part of the contents of your mind is the sensory data coming into your brain from your body. When you take ketamine, your awareness of that connection is temporarily dampened because ketamine is—once again—an anesthetic. What you have left is a totally non-ordinary state of mind. To some, that can feel like "losing your mind." All that's really happening, however, is that you have dissociated from the sense of your bodily self. You are a "self" without a body at that point. For people who, for whatever reason, dissociate regularly, this will likely feel familiar, and be very pleasant and easy. On the other hand, for those of us who tighten up and hunker down to deal with stress, it can be uncomfortable— and take some getting used to. Once you get used to dissociation though, it's a very valuable place to go.

DISSOCIATIVE

➤ASSOCIATIVE◄

In contrast, here's what happens on traditional psychedelics. You still lose your mind, as a result of being unable to direct your focus in a normal way, but you also keep receiving sense data from your body. This can make the experience extremely physically intense. Practically speaking, this means that anywhere your mind goes, the energetic state of your body will follow. If you see or remember something overwhelming from the past, it will again feel overwhelming because the brain will automatically bring the body back into the high-energy state associated with that memory.

I like to say that traditional psychedelics are reassociative, meaning they bring you back to past experiences in their full glory—or terror, as the case may be. Traditional psychedelics help (again, perhaps force) you to experience the physical arousal associated with some past event plus all the thoughts, emotions, and stories you have in your mind about that event. Unfortunately, if you haven't practiced being comfortable with a very high energy state in your body—and if you aren't comfortable with expressing that energy in movement and sound as the medicine "takes charge," as I like to say—this could feel extremely overwhelming to you and potentially create an intensely negative experience.

Conversely, ketamine facilitates disconnection of the story of what happened from the emotionally aroused experience of it. You can deeply observe the past timeline in a state of complete calm. Once you've had an experience of visiting that past story without the emotional overwhelm, you'll be on your way to resolving that pain or trauma.

Now let's visit the situation where dissociation can be "bad." "Bad" dissociation happens when the emotion of an experience and the storyline are separated automatically by the brain during the event in order to protect you from what it believes is too much to handle. That's a good thing at the time, but turns into a bad thing when emotional arousal starts happening later at seemingly random or inappropriate moments.

This actually happens to all of us, all the time—it's how our brains work—but it's generally so minor that we simply call it "normal emotional reactions." Side note: There is actually no such thing as an emotional "reaction," because that's not how our brains function. I'm using the colloquialism for ease of reading, but please know, the phrase "emotional reaction" is just a popular term based on a fiction of how the brain works.

To illustrate the point simply, one of the most dramatic examples of dissociation gone bad is when a former soldier "returns to combat" mentally and physically at the sound of fireworks or other loud bangs. Typically, this person has never expressed and cannot express feelings in connection with the events of their overwhelming combat situation. But an unexpected loud sound will set off a cascade of out-of-context behaviors within them.

What happens at the moment of the sound is that the soldier's brain conjures up a past wartime scene, and—in the way brains are supposed to work, only gone awry—has simultaneously put their body into the energetically aroused physical state appropriate to that past scene. He or she is carried away by actions appropriate to that memory as if it were happening "right now."

There are two possible routes to resolving this dilemma. One is to dissociate the sound of a bang from its physical correlates via a ketamine experience. The other is to relive it all at once—both the memory of the event and the unpleasant high energy—under the influence of a traditional psychedelic, which is generally much more subjectively difficult.

According to research, changing your brain functioning so you get the mental health changes you want means you'll have to take doses that make you "let go" of the normal way you experience your body.[2] For some, that will be comfortable, even pleasant. For others, it might be difficult at first.

YOU SIMPLY HAVE TO REMEMBER THAT BEING UNTETHERED FROM YOUR ORDINARY PERCEPTION OF PHYSICAL REALITY DOES NOT MEAN YOU'RE UNSAFE.

What if, while on ketamine, you uncover something bad that you didn't know you didn't know?

There's no getting around it. It is possible—though not probable—that you discover something "bad" during one of your experiences. You might also discover the details of something bad you already know happened to you. This does not mean, however, that you will learn details if you don't want to.

I have a patient who began her journey with a desire to not remember any details of something she knows happened to her, and in more than a dozen ketamine experiences, she has not. Another patient of mine thought she needed to know details of something bad that had happened, and discovered that it doesn't matter what the details are. For her, seeing flashes of a particular time in childhood and knowing that whatever happened left her feeling weird is enough. There are no certainties about what you'll see, and your intention will often dictate what appears.

While under the influence of ketamine, anything "bad" you discover will not bring physically overwhelming symptoms. Remember that since it's an anesthetic, ketamine induces a state of the body that mitigates energetic arousal (including arousal derived from categorically unpleasant new information).

You might have heard the unfortunate story of Tim Ferriss realizing via psychedelics that he was molested from the age of two until he was four. (For the record, the psychedelics in question were of the classical variety, not ketamine.)

This is a perfect example of one of the reasons why ketamine is the best place to start in the world of deep-dive psychedelics. Under ketamine, suppressed unpleasant memories will be something you become aware of dispassionately as they arise, without the freak-out Ferriss describes. A physical feeling of terror, trauma, or overwhelm simply won't occur. Once the medicine wears off, you remain in the headspace, and physical state, of calm observation rather than one of overarousal.

I'VE SAID IT BEFORE, BUT IT BEARS REPEATING. CALM OBSERVATION IS THE FIRST PART OF ANY LASTING TRAUMA RESOLUTION. At that point, deeply in a ketamine-induced state of plasticity, you'll be able to reach for your community or your therapist to talk, understand, get new perspective, or anything else to help integrate the painful truth you've uncovered into the arc of your life story in a meaningful way.

Ketamine could well lead you to the discovery of something highly unpleasant about yourself, those you love, your past, or your present. **REST ASSURED, THOUGH, THE KETAMINE EXPERIENCE AND THE POST-KETAMINE BRAIN SPACE ARE THE BEST POSSIBLE PLACES FROM WHICH TO START ADDRESSING ANY REVELATIONS YOU WEREN'T EXPECTING.**

chapter 5

Ketamine and Your Real Life

You're still here? Well done, you!

While I've got you, here's my final pitch for ketamine-assisted therapy: While being an extremely efficient, direct way to building self-awareness and reaching your mental health goals, the benefits do not stop there.

Let's say you're a freelance entrepreneur. You're not doing the typical 9-to-5 shtick where you're someone's employee and you passively show up at the office every day. You're hustling! You're getting a gig here, and another gig there.

Before you got there, you had to go through the terror that is taking the leap from employee to business owner. How long did that take? How much anguish did you go through? The fears you had probably wouldn't have qualified as mental health struggles, but they sure held you back from taking chances that, looking back, you know you could have taken sooner. What if you had been able to engage in a practice of **LETTING GO INTO THE UNCERTAINTY OF YOUR FUTURE** so that process took you two years instead of six?

The beauty of ketamine is that getting good at letting go is a much shorter process than the one you might go through as you become a successful entrepreneur. In two hours, you'll be able to experience what it feels like to really "let go." At first, it might feel weird and confusing, even awful. You might spend the whole experience fighting that feeling tooth and nail. It could take many ketamine experiences to learn to let go with ease. But once you do, it'll be very pleasant. And that translates to "letting go" more easily in real life.

Even if you're not an entrepreneur, being able to "let go" is important.

UNCERTAINTY
becomes

FAMILIAR and
LESS UNCOMFORTABLE

Being able to "let go" translates to a diminished fear of dying. It translates into an understanding of your place in the universe, which won't make sense until you've had the experience, so pardon the woo-woo moment there. But "letting go" is a real experience that makes a tangible difference in your everyday life. Being able to let go also translates into comfort with uncertainty. You spend less—if any—time mired in needless existential worry. There's more time for enjoyment or productive action. Letting go can become so familiar to your brain that it allows you to let go with ease the next time life is pressing on you to loosen your grip.

Translation: Life feels easier and more pleasant.

It's not so important to comprehend your psychedelic experiences in some concrete way. Like dreams, they can be pretty abstract. Focus your intent instead on exploring the associations you have with your thoughts and feelings. This practice forms the nuts and bolts of building your self-awareness.

EXPLORE
the associations you have to your thoughts and feelings

From self-awareness, you can move to self-transformation through integration—either in a group setting or working individually with a supportive mental health professional. Integration works best when you:

Learn new ways to manipulate the levers of your nervous system

Absorb new concepts through which you can understand your experiences (both new and old)

Truly belong in a safe community where you can share / discuss / ask questions

The point of going through ketamine therapy is not the molecule itself—it's the integration. Ketamine, like any psychedelic, gets you to the threshold of dealing with challenges in a new way.

IT'S TEMPTING TO THINK OF KETAMINE AS A GOLDEN TICKET, OR MAGIC PILL. BUT REALLY, KETAMINE IS JUST A GATEWAY TO THE POSSIBILITY OF TRANSFORMATION.

To say it another way, psychedelic experiences are useful in that they can enhance the ways that therapy has always helped.

By getting you to try something different than your modus operandi.

By helping you think in new ways.

By teaching you new methods for pulling the levers on your mood.

By helping you practice new ways to show up in your relationships with friends, family, and lovers.

A friend and colleague told me that ketamine has been a powerful tool in her journey to cultivate open-mindedness towards new learning and behaviors. For her, the opening of her mind meant she could set aside biases toward self-marketing and take steps to build her online visibility. For someone else, it might be learning that you can be more than what you've told yourself you can be for your whole life.

Do I really need to go through the integration process?

Like everything else in life, you get out of ketamine-assisted therapy what you put into it. If all you want is to temporarily reduce inflammation, modulate your immune system, and clear out cortisol; by all means skip the integration. If you truly believe that you don't need to capitalize on the brain changes that have occurred, or change any of the concepts that you rely on to understand yourself and the world, I guess you can do it by yourself, that's fine. But if you're the kind of self-aware and determined person who goes to the effort of pursuing ketamine in the first place, I doubt you'll be satisfied with just a quick, temporary, biochemical fix.

Maybe the community that surrounds you is not optimal. Maybe the lens through which you see yourself and others is not as pleasant as it could realistically be. Maybe your ketamine journey comes with a side dish of resolving trauma or dealing with abandonment. By skipping the integration, you are missing out on rare opportunities to—pardon my French—resolve more of your s**t.

All of us have those petty annoyances that don't noticeably affect our day-to-day life, but are bringing us down in invisible ways. Most of us will not get opportunities to definitively unravel these unresolved problems.

You can manage the symptoms of inflammation, immune dysfunction, and chronically elevated cortisol until you're blue in the face (or, until your doctor won't prescribe you any more ketamine). But if you want real, lasting, positive change in your life, you need the integration process.

AS THE WORD IMPLIES, INTEGRATION BRINGS TOGETHER ALL THE PIECES OF THIS SUPERCHARGED DOSE OF SELF-AWARENESS.

Without integration, you get relief from physiological symptoms. With integration, you create the space needed for personal transformation. People who integrate develop autonomy. People who don't integrate risk developing a "habit" with ketamine.

INTEGRATION
autonomy independence wellness

vs.

NO INTEGRATION
you risk developing a ketamine habit

Do I need to change therapists in order to do ketamine-assisted therapy?

That depends entirely on whether or not your therapist is afraid of what you're doing.

Your therapist needs to:

- Understand why you're seeking out ketamine-assisted therapy

- Understand that you're safe using the medicine

- Trust your judgment on what's best for you and your mental health

- Be eager to facilitate the work of your transformation

- Be comfortable helping you integrate mystical / spiritual / transpersonal / experiences

If your therapist has no knowledge of or experience with ketamine or other psychedelics, you'll absolutely need guidance from someone who can help you understand practical, physiological aspects of your experiences with ketamine (the molecule). Aside from that and the above caveats, feel free to keep up your relationship with the person who knows you best. I say that because many therapists, even without having had a medicine-facilitated psychedelic journey themselves, can easily help you understand and integrate mystical / spiritual / transpersonal / peak experiences. Many people (therapists included) have had these types of experiences without ever taking psychedelics.[1]

How many doses does it take to "complete" a ketamine journey?

Don't hate me, but the answer is: a very unsatisfying "It depends." Often when we're stuck in long-term unpleasantness (whether of low or high arousal), it's a result of tissue damage or inflammation. For a lot of people who are in severe mental health situations, the reality is that their body's energy budgets are very out of whack—and have been for months or years.

There are some people who have a semi-miraculous recovery after one dose of ketamine. What happens there is not well understood. However, there is research showing that at a dissociative dose, a regrowth of connections between brain cells occurs in many people, and that this "increase in synaptic density" is correlated with a rapid resolution of treatment-resistant depression.[2]

In others with less treatment-resistant depression, the brain's cells begin "talking" to each other more efficiently, which is also correlated with a rapid decrease in depressive symptoms.[3]

This is my conjecture about what else is going on: in some people, ketamine's anti-inflammatory action dramatically dials down inflammation so they begin to feel fundamentally more pleasant. Remember mood and core affect from earlier? A shift of mood/core affect to a more pleasant valence automatically translates into less depressive symptoms. For other people, that alteration in brain chemistry takes four, six, or eight doses (during a timeframe within which ketamine's effects are continuous enough that inflammation stays low).

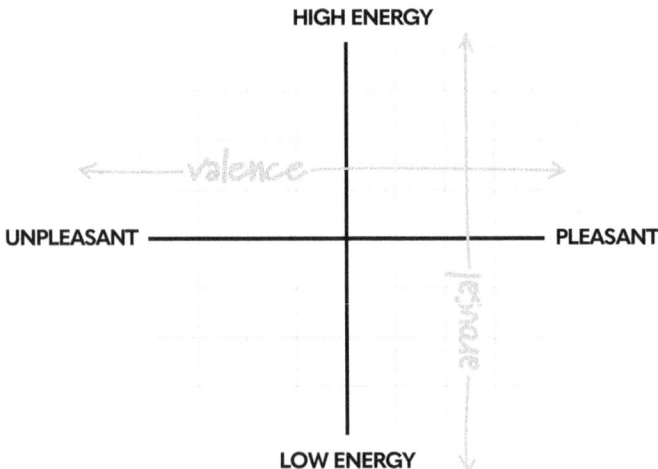

HIGH ENERGY

valence

UNPLEASANT ——————————————— PLEASANT

arousal

LOW ENERGY

When we feel pleasant physiologically, we do pleasant things. We think pleasant thoughts. We see the world as a pleasant place. When your body is in a more pleasant state (as far as repair of tissue damage and inflammation goes), if your past experience has any sort of positivity in it, that's where you'll go in your mindset.

So, back to the question of how long it takes for ketamine to "work" in a definite way. If you've been in a very deep hole mentally for some time, very likely you're also in a deep hole physically, and your brain is stuck in that old story. The more frequently you do ketamine, the faster it can help lift you out of that hole.

It is also possible that the process to extract yourself from your hole is more short-term because you aren't in too deep. In that case, you'd have a short initial journey. Later, life circumstances might send you in a more inflammatory or depressed direction, at which point you could decide to revisit ketamine.

Or perhaps a recovery from tissue damage is taking longer than you expected because your brain is stuck in a loop where you feel you're in pain, even when there's nothing actually going on in your nerves. A single ketamine experience might give your brain new synaptic connections to get you out of said hole like "Boom!" (I'm not exaggerating; it really can be that fast.)

PHYSICAL
inflammation
tissue damage
c o r t i s o l

VS.

MENTAL
c o n c e p t s
stuck in a loop

Then there are those of us who have low-grade chronic tension from the concepts we're carrying around in our heads, or from the way society happens to categorize us. I'm going to level with you: Ketamine is going to take longer in your case AND you'll need to do at least one of these two things.

1. Meaningfully involve yourself in a relationship or community (therapeutic or otherwise) that regards you with compassionate curiosity

2. Proactively fill your head with new, constructive concepts about who you are and how you can negotiate the world as it is

Something interesting I've seen repeatedly is that a person will have a ketamine experience so unpleasant that they're not sure they really want to keep going. If they do decide to push forward anyway, that's precisely when the clouds lift. I've seen it happen after someone has an unexpected mystical experience. I've seen it happen after someone returns to normal consciousness, unable to remember anything of the experience. I've even seen it after someone has a very unpleasant experience of mild nausea and dizziness for up to 24 hours after a return to normal consciousness. In each of these cases, clarity and change subsequently came rapidly.

As I've mentioned, the dissociative experience is the point at which dramatic brain changes occur, but a gradual process can also be occurring in the background. It can seem like there's no change for a while, but "all of a sudden" things begin to shift. The buildup of changes below your level of conscious awareness cascades into a perceptibly more pleasant feeling in daily life.

For some people, that point is three doses. For others, it's eight doses. For still others, it's 15 doses. It really depends on how stuck and rigid the prior patterns were, and how diminished brain cell density and communication are. Not to mention the ongoing state of the body's energy budget.

Most people will need to go to the deeply dissociated place where the "magic" happens at least once, if not repeatedly. They'll need the brain growth and connections that occur at that threshold for any changes to even begin.

Some are lucky enough to feel drastically better after just one session. The inflammation, tissue damage, and cortisol get cleared, and the person just feels that everything has changed.

99% of us need to go through a process of changing the concepts we use to navigate life before we feel improvements.

Repetition with frequency and duration are necessary for you to apply new concepts to your life: to the acceptance of loss, to the understanding of your own response to that loss, to adapting how you approach your family dynamics, etc. So, once again, don't leave out the integration and involvement in a relationship or community (therapeutic or otherwise) that actually facilitates new thinking and new experiences.

When you talk about tissue damage, do you mean folks suffering from chronic pain?

Yes. Often, chronic pain arises from an accident or illness that caused tissue or nerve damage. For example; postherpetic neuralgia[4] (a lasting pain in the healed skin areas where you had shingles), phantom limb pain[5] (amputated limbs), chronic migraine, or back pain. The current understanding of chronic pain, based on brain function, goes a little something like this: The tissue or nerve damage has actually been healed, but the brain is still stuck in the pain loop.

You see, the brain works by predicting what will happen in your immediate future based on your past experiences in similar contexts.[6] One more time for the people in the back: The brain does not react to what is really happening. The brain anticipates the next moment based on what has already happened.

The brains of people with chronic pain are effectively creating a subjective experience of tissue damage that no longer exists. Those people are living in a loop that their brains have been stuck in since the tissue damage first occurred. The brain has neither learned nor encoded the novel sensory information that the tissue damage is actually resolved.

There is no pain signal from the relevant part of the body. Not to say that the pain is all in your head, because you're really experiencing the pain. And if you have chronic pain, I want to emphasize that this is not at all your fault. You're being victimized by how the brain works.

But here's the upshot. Ketamine has the capacity to help create new synaptic connections that can break your brain out of that loop. As I've mentioned, it takes energy to learn. If you've undergone tissue damage, your body has spent a lot of energy and nutritional resources on healing that tissue damage. One of the many useful things ketamine does is that it gives you a little extra energy. This effect won't last forever, but it will temporarily put you in a position to eat better, to exercise, to stop hanging out with those "friends" who make you hate yourself.

KETAMINE SUPPORTS YOUR CAPACITY TO MAKE BETTER CHOICES. Those improved choices will boost your body's energy budget so that you can help your brain get out of any irrelevant loops it might be stuck in.

Are there people for whom ketamine doesn't work?

There is some data floating around that for about 20% of people, ketamine does not work. But to my mind, it is important to circle back to these questions: How bad is the chronic inflammation? If neuroplasticity is what facilitates success, how many doses or how deep an experience is needed to get any particular person to a state of neuroplasticity?

If you're dealing with a body-budget problem so fundamental that you need to completely overhaul your diet and sleep habits, then ketamine might not seem to be working for you yet.

You might need to regress before you can progress. Yes, there are definitely people who've done 10 or 15 doses who still aren't progressing. Those people will probably want to consult with their prescriber about their dose, and perhaps need to dial their problem-solving back to sleep and food. Ketamine is an incredibly effective piece of the puzzle, but it's not a panacea. Good food, sleep, and movement can be applied every single day. If ketamine doesn't seem to be working on you, go back to those daily basics.

Choose what you can afford. Choose one that's nearby. If at all possible, choose a company that includes an integration process as part of the program, or at the very least has a relationship with therapists or mental health coaches.

Again, you can go to a clinic for the physiological benefits and management of physical symptoms. But if you're still not getting mental health symptom relief, or the experiences feel bad, you might need to dial into the whole integration side of things.

For someone who holds on to control to maintain a sense of stability and feels comfortable anchored in the physical reality of their body, ketamine's ability to make you totally "let go" is likely to make you think, temporarily, that you've lost your mind. It might even make you think that you've died.

Sounds terrifying, I know. But thankfully
-*the worry doesn't last.*
-*you don't care once it happens.*
-*now you know the secret.*

There's immense value in "totally losing control" while knowing that everything's fine — or learning through repeated experiences of "letting go" that everything is fine once you do.

You also now know there are positive effects of lower ketamine doses that accumulate after several sessions: anti-inflammation, immune modulation, clearing your cortisol levels, etc. Along with these benefits, lower doses create a trancelike state which allows you, in a therapy setting, to talk more easily about things that have been traditionally difficult to talk about. Ketamine removes the physical discomfort of stories and emotional experiences so you can speak about them without overwhelm.

This is great news, because therapists and neuropsychiatrists alike agree that a huge piece of processing and recovering from trauma is separating out the physical aspects of an over-aroused nervous system from the story. Ketamine is perfectly poised to help you move forward from these difficulties much faster.

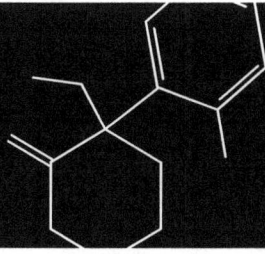

The last and most important

thing to remember is that chasing symptom relief is not the point. If you don't have a program of building self-awareness, that's all you're doing.

IF YOU GAIN JUST ONE THING FROM THIS BOOK, LET IT BE THIS:

Should you embark on a ketamine journey for mental health, make sure you also engage in a program for integrating and amplifying the self-awareness you've begun.

That can be a course like The Feel Good Formula® I developed, an ongoing connection with a therapist, life coach, spiritual guide, or whatever else works for you, in either an individual or group setting. This choice will be key to an end goal of feeling more pleasant than unpleasant, more of the time, no matter what other specific goals you're looking to achieve in your life.

Bon Voyage!

ACKNOWLEDGEMENTS

The value to humanity of non-ordinary states of consciousness dates back to thousands of years before the birth of Christ, as documented in Brian Muraresku's book, The Immortality Key. I am grateful for the courageous individuals who worked to bring this value into the modern day, so ordinary people can responsibly improve their mental health. A non-exhaustive list includes Albert Hofmann, Ph.D., Carl A.P. Ruck, Ph.D., R. Gordon Wasson, Aldous Huxley, James Fadiman, Ph.D., William A. Richards, Ph.D., Roland R. Griffiths, Ph.D., Rick Strassman, M.D., Rick Doblin, Ph.D., Paul Stamets, Stan Grof, M.D., and so many others. I am also grateful for the bravery of the many unnamed guides and therapists who worked underground, helping people use psychedelics for mental health since the end of legal use in 1971. Without their collective wisdom and experience, the existing problem of limited access to these valuable tools for healing would be compounded.

In 1933, Wilhelm Reich, M.D., (the father of body-based psychotherapy) wrote,

> **❝** It is, therefore, to be expected that biopsychiatry will sooner or later succeed in describing human structures and characteristic reactions in terms of bioenergetic metabolism, emotional tolerance of biophysical excitation, and capacity for energy discharge. Such an energetic point of view would enable us to handle, finally, human nature, not with complicated ideas and experiences, but with simple energy functions, as we are handling the rest of nature. **❞**

simple energy functions

I am grateful to Lisa Feldman Barrett, Ph.D., for having achieved this task. With the Theory of Constructed Emotion, she has created a paradigm shift in the way we understand emotions. Instead of outdated theories that have now been rendered fictions, the theory of constructed emotion rises solidly from the latest data on brain function. Consequently, it is now possible to understand emotions in terms of simple energy function. This foundation also makes it possible to understand—simply and practically— psychedelics as a valuable asset to humanity in its search for healing.

I am grateful to the guides and mentors I've encountered on my ketamine and psychedelic journey thus far. Some of these people I have met personally, some I am separated from by time or distance. Their experience and testimonies have given me the courage to pursue psychedelics as a tool for not only going deeper on my own odyssey of the mind, but also as a way of facilitating the journeys of those who come to me for assistance. Among these guides and mentors are Richard Brandt, Phil Wolfson M.D., Kate Yeadaker, A.P.R.N., Karl L. R. Jansen, M.D., Ph.D., John C. Lilly, M.D., Alexander "Sasha" Shulgin, Ph.D., Carl L. Hart, Ph.D., William James, M.D., Humphry Osmond, M.R.C.S., D.P.M., Abram Hoffer, M.D., Ph.D., and William ("Bill W.") Griffith Wilson.

I might not be traveling this path at all if not for Kazi "Zayn" Hassan, M.D., and Kabir Ali, co-founders of My Ketamine Home, a telemedicine ketamine-for-mental-health program based in Florida. I am deeply grateful to them for first introducing me to the safety and efficacy of ketamine for mental health. From that point, I quickly gained confidence in the combined efficacy of ketamine and the depth and body-based psychology I practice to facilitate rapid results for clients. I am also deeply grateful to Hassan and Ali for inviting me to serve as the subject matter expert in psychotherapy and affording me the opportunity to develop the integration program for Nue Life Health, the startup that bought and expanded their company. Those experiences formed a key basis of my drive to write this book.

I'm grateful to the family, friends, and colleagues who have generously given time and attention to my obsessive discussions and exploration of the topic. It was with their encouragement that I decided to write this book.

Last but not least, I am grateful to my editors (Helen Hope, Reina Dorado, and Sonia Davis), the readers who helped make sure I didn't overlook anything, my designer Amy Gindhart, and my Last Mile Publishing concierge, Bill Bonney.

GLOSSARY

ANESTHETIC - Anesthetics are a diverse group of drugs used in the management of pain. Ketamine is a dissociative anesthetic. Since it's an anesthetic, ketamine induces a state of the body that mitigates energetic arousal, including arousal derived from categorically unpleasant new information.

AROUSAL - I don't mean sexual arousal. In this context, arousal is science-speak for high energy. Energetic activation. The opposite of fatigue.

ASSOCIATIVE - Traditional psychedelics are associative in nature, as they do not dissociate or separate you from the sensations in your body the way ketamine does. During a traditional psychedelic experience, whatever is happening in your mind can influence your body, and vice versa. Associative psychedelics connect or associate your mind and your body. Refer to: PSYCHEDELICS, TRADITIONAL.

BODY BUDGET or **BODY'S ENERGY BUDGET** - The dynamic process your brain engages in 24/7 to manage energy resources in your body. The scientific term for this is allostasis. The metaphor of a body budget was developed by Lisa Feldman Barrett, PhD.

BRAIN PLASTICITY - Refer to: NEUROPLASTICITY

CATEGORY - A collection of objects, events, or actions grouped together as equivalent for some purpose. (Lisa Feldman Barrett, How Emotions are Made, 2018, page 87)

CONCEPT - Mental representation of a category. (Lisa Feldman Barrett, How Emotions are Made, 2018, page 87)

CONTRACTED - In the context of mental activity, the term explains the phenomenon of a "flashlight"-like quality of attention versus a "lantern"-like quality. As in the heart's expansion and contraction to circulate blood, and the lungs' expansion and contraction as we breathe, life goals are better served by thinking that can be either tight and focused or broad and open-minded. A contracted mind generally correlates with a ready-for-action (aroused) state of the nervous system.

DEEP DIVE - Refer to: MYSTICAL EXPERIENCE

DISSOCIATIVE - A state of mind not integrated with the sensations in your body. Ketamine, for example, dissociates conscious awareness from the sensations in the body. This is very helpful in mental health therapy addressing PTSD or trauma. In resolving PTSD and trauma, strong feelings can come up in the body that are subjectively overwhelming and thus very difficult to heal. Ketamine's dissociative quality makes this healing process much easier. Refer to: ASSOCIATIVE.

EGO - Your identity as _____. For example: your identity as a spouse, a parent, a loser, a winner, a scrappy hard worker, victim, etc. Identification with whatever concepts you use to understand who you are, including your identity as a person.

EGO DEATH - Letting go of your identity as _____. For example: letting go of your identity as a person, or any of the other identities you carry with you.

EMOTIONS - Emotions are concepts. They are meanings you assign in a particular context and based on past experience, to the combination of sensory data from inside your body and sensory data from outside your body.

ENCODING PREDICTION ERROR - This phrase is the fancy, scientific way to say, "learning." For example, you're playing a game and you have predicted all the things you need to do to hit that ball. But then you miss it! Drat!! So you begin the process of encoding this prediction error and trying again to hit the ball.

EXPERIENCE - The time period when you're under the influence of ketamine.

EXPANSIVE - In the context of mental activity, "expansive" explains the phenomenon of a more "lantern"-like quality of attention versus a "flashlight"-like quality. Like the heart's expansion and contraction to circulate blood, and the lungs' expansion and contraction as we breathe, life goals are better served by thinking that can be both tight and focused as well as broad and open-minded. An expansive mind generally correlates with a relaxed (quiescent) state of the nervous system.

FIGHT-OR-FLIGHT - Refer to: SYMPATHETIC ACTIVATION.

GLUTAMATE - An "excitatory" neurotransmitter (brain chemical) that plays a key role in learning and memory. It creates the right "chemical soup" in your brain to help you reach your mental health goals faster.

HALLUCINATION - A potential occurrence while under the influence of ketamine. Hallucinations are sensory experiences that are very real to the person having them, but not real to anyone else. With ketamine, hallucinations are typically visual and sometimes auditory. Under the influence of ketamine, hallucinations are most often experienced as dreamlike visuals that happen while you are awake. Technically, they are visual representations of sensory data from your surroundings and your body that are combined in the moment with old information stored in your brain. Sometimes, these are simply a replay of elements of your everyday life.

HYPERAROUSAL - Excessively energetic in either a pleasant or unpleasant way. Can be a symptom of chronic low-grade fight-or-flight, aka: chronic stress and PTSD.

INTEGRATION - The process of applying and practicing what you have learned in ketamine-assisted therapy in a discerning way.

JOURNEY - The whole process of ketamine-assisted therapy.

KETAMINE - A general anesthetic currently being used off-label for treatment-resistant depression and other mental health matters. One product (Spravato® (esketamine) nasal spray) has been FDA approved for treatment-resistant depression. Being an anesthetic, ketamine dissociates you from the sensations in your body during your experience. This is in opposition to traditional psychedelics, which have no anesthetic qualities. The dissociative nature of ketamine makes it very helpful in addressing PTSD and traumatic memories without the negative side effect of overarousal. Ketamine is a non-traditional psychedelic. Refer to: PSYCHEDELICS, TRADITIONAL.

K-HOLE - Refer to: MYSTICAL EXPERIENCE.

MENTAL HEALTH DOSE - Specific dosing (here, of ketamine) to optimize mental health benefits.

MYSTICAL EXPERIENCE - "...*Mystical has nothing to do with states of mind that are misty or vague. Nor does the term refer to magic or usual occult or paranormal phenomena. Rather this term denotes a form of consciousness that vividly remains in the memory banks of those who witness it. All of the great world religions have words that point toward this highly desired and valued state of spiritual awareness, such as samadhi in Hinduism, nirvana in Buddhism, sekhel mufla in Judaism, the beatific vision in Christianity, baqá wa faná in Islam, and wu wei in Taoism.*"
- Excerpt from Sacred Knowledge by William A. Richards, Ph.D.

NEURAL PLASTICITY - Refer to: NEUROPLASTICITY

NEUROPLASTICITY - A brain state that optimizes potential for learning.

NMDA RECEPTORS - N-methyl D-aspartate receptors, which are involved in learning and memory and affected by ketamine.

NON-ORDINARY STATE OF CONSCIOUSNESS (NOSC) - An altered state of consciousness, such as during a dream state, hallucinations, meditations, trance, or hypnosis. It's a nice, neutral description of what you are experiencing while "tripping."

OVERAROUSAL - More energy in your body than the current situation calls for. Usually feels unpleasant.

PARASYMPATHETIC - There are two branches of your autonomic nervous system: one for action (spending energy) and one for relaxing (saving or preserving energy). The parasympathetic branch regulates relaxation. When you hear "rest-and-digest," they're talking about the parasympathetic branch of the autonomic nervous system. Bottom line, it's all about relaxing. You know you are getting more "parasympathetic" if any of the following things are happening: more saliva, watery eyes, a need to pee or poo, or digestion. You'll also just feel more relaxed when you are "getting parasympathetic."

PSYCHEDELIC - Mind manifesting or mind revealing. From Greek "psykhē" meaning mind or soul, and "dēloun" meaning to manifest or reveal.

PSYCHEDELICS, TRADITIONAL - Typically, these substances keep you consciously connected to or associated with the sensations in your body while you're under their influence. This is in contrast to ketamine, which, being an anesthetic, dissociates or disconnects you from the sensations in your body during your experience. Traditional psychedelics interact with serotonin receptors in your brain and include LSD, psilocybin, mescaline, ayahuasca, and DMT. Ketamine, on the other hand, has a different mechanism of action and interacts with glutamate receptors.

SELF-AWARENESS - The continuous process of becoming aware of your blind spots i.e. the stuff you don't know about yourself.

SELF-TRANSFORMATION - Making changes to yourself.

SENSE DATA - Sensory information your brain receives from inside your body or outside your body, whether or not you're consciously aware of that information.

SET AND SETTING - Your mindset and the environment you are in during a psychedelic experience.

SHADOW SELF - Your unconscious mind. Refer to: UNCONSCIOUS.

SPIRITUAL - A less physically contracted, less focused mental and physical state. Under the influence of ketamine, your body will be free of the typical contractions it holds so that you can get things done (remember, it's an anesthetic). Because of that, you will be experiencing the world through a more expansive, non-ordinary (for you) lens. This lens is "spiritual." Under this definition, sleep and dreaming are both spiritual experiences. So, if you don't consider yourself a "spiritual" person, think of the sleep state to help you understand the term in a more concrete way.

SYMPATHETIC ACTIVATION OR AROUSAL - There are two branches of your autonomic nervous system: one for action (spending energy) and one for relaxing (saving or preserving energy). The sympathetic branch is for action. The most common label for it is the "fight-or-flight" branch (which is in large part a misnomer, but that's a story for another time). You know you're getting more "sympathetic" if any of the following things are happening: you feel super energetic, your mouth goes dry, you need to pee or poo but can't, you're short of breath, you feel panicky, your mind is racing, you're jittery, you feel worked up. Bottom line, it's all about action.

TISSUE DAMAGE - The literal, physical damage to tissues or organs of your body.

TRANSFORMATION - The process of completing personal changes and achieving goals.

TRANSPERSONAL - Happening outside of the body. Transpersonality is completely conceptual because it refers to the self "as spirit." In other words, it's not about anything real in the sense of things that have "matter" as part of their identity (like being a human with a body). Transpersonal describes the exploration of ideas of self without identification as a body and the experience of being a part of the "connected whole" of "all that is."

In everyday life, your body is the vehicle through which you relate to this world. When you lose your identification with your body, you're "experiencing" on a more transpersonal level. Detachment from the body is heightened with ketamine, and facilitates what some call a "transpersonal" experience. This is simply another word to describe a mystical or spiritual experience. Refer to: MYSTICAL EXPERIENCE

Throughout your journey with psychedelics, you might find ideas from transpersonal psychology useful to help you make sense of any experiences that are hard to put into everyday words.

TRIP - A colloquial term for a psychedelic experience. Often the term of choice for people using psychedelics on a recreational basis.

UNCONSCIOUS - Patterns of actions or thought not in your conscious awareness at the moment. Some unconscious material can be easily accessed with focused conscious attention. Other unconscious material requires a long period of self observation, reflections from others, and/or psychedelic experiences to access. The bulk of your unconscious about yourself and how relationships work was formed in the first seven years of your life.

NOTES

Chapter 1

1. C.A. Zarate Jr., R. Machado-Vieira, "Ketamine: translating mechanistic discoveries into the next generation of glutamate modulators for mood disorders," Nature, 2017 JAN 10, https://www.nature.com/articles/mp2016249

2. G. Mion, "History of anaesthesia, The ketamine story – past, present and future," European Journal of Anaesthesiology, 2017 SEP, https://journals.lww.com/ejanaesthesiology/fulltext/2017/09000/history_of_anaesthesia__the_ketamine_story___past,.2.aspx

3. M.S. Kurdi, K.A. Theerth, R.S. Deva, "Ketamine: Current applications in anesthesia, pain, and critical care," NIH National Library of Medicine, 2014 SEP-DEC, https://www.ncbi.nlm.nih.gov/pmc/articles/PMC4258981/

4. R. Haridy, "Psychedelic Medicine 101: The curious case of ketamine," New Atlas, 2018 JUN 12, https://newatlas.com/psychedelic-medicine-ketamine/54970/

Chapter 2

1. K. Killinger, D. McPhillips, "Ketamine infusions improve symptoms of depression, anxiety and suicidal ideation, study says," CNN, 2022 SEPT 12, https://www.cnn.com/2022/09/12/health/ketamine-infusions-help-depression-study-wellness/index.html

2. D. Souery, G.I. Papakostas, M.H. Trivedi, "Treatment-Resistant Depression," Journal of Clinical Psychiatry 2006 Volume 67 Supplement 6, https://www.psychiatrist.com/read-pdf/21622/

3. M. Callahan, "Your Brain is the World's Most Proficient Accountant. Here's How," News@Northeastern, 2020 DEC 1, https://news.northeastern.edu/2020/12/01/your-brain-is-the-worlds-most-proficient-accountant-heres-how/

4. T. White, "K for OCD," Stanford Medicine Magazine, 2017 AUG 17, https://stanmed.stanford.edu/carolyn-rodriguez-ketamine-ocd/

5. A. Georgiou, "What Is Ketamine Used for Medically? Alcoholism Could Be Next for Drug After Promising Study," Newsweek, 2022 JAN 22, https://www.newsweek.com/what-ketamine-used-medically-alcoholism-next-drug-promising-study-mental-health-addiction-1668547

6. R.K. Das, G. Gale, K. Walsh, V.E. Hennessy, G. Iskandar, L.A. Mordecai, B. Brandner, M. Kindt, H.V. Curran, S.K. Kamboj, "Ketamine can reduce harmful drinking by pharmacologically rewriting drinking memories," Nature, 2019 NOV 26, https://www.nature.com/articles/s41467-019-13162-w

7. C. Mallenbaum, A. Rivas, E. Goldberg, J. Ackermann, A. Valenski, "Are Psychedelics the Future of Eating Disorder Treatments?" theSkimm', 2022 JUN 8, https://www.theskimm.com/wellness/disordered-eating-psychedelics?utm_source=newsletter_ds&utm_medium=email

8. L.F. Barrett, "Your Brain Is Not for Thinking," The New York Times, 2020 NOV 23, https://www.nytimes.com/2020/11/23/opinion/brain-neuroscience-stress.html

9. R. Ostroff, J.S. Kothari, "Reversal of Non-Suppression of Cortisol Levels in a Patient With Refractory Depression Receiving Ketamine," The American Journal of Psychiatry, 2015 JAN 01, https://ajp.psychiatryonline.org/doi/10.1176/appi.ajp.2014.14060776

10. L.F. Barrett, "Seven and a Half Lessons About the Brain," New York, Houghton Mifflin Harcourt Publishing Company, 2020, page 9.

Chapter 3

1. A. Wells, "Benzodiazepines and Alcohol and their effect on ketamine treatments," American Society of Ketamine Physicians (ASKP), https://www.askp.org/benzodiazepines-and-alcohol-and-their-effect-on-ketamine-treatments/

2. K. Jansen, "Ketamine: Dreams and Realities," Santa Cruz: Multidisciplinary Association for Psychedelic Studies (MAPS), 2004, page 283

3. R.M. Berman, A. Cappiello, A. Anand, D.A. Oren, G.R. Heninger, D.S. Charney, J.H. Krystal, "Antidepressant effects of ketamine in depressed patients," Biol Psychiatry, 2000 FEB 15, https://pubmed.ncbi.nlm.nih.gov/10686270/

4. K. Hassan, W.M. Struthers, A. Sankarabhotla, P. Davis, "Safety, effectiveness and tolerability of sublingual ketamine in depression and anxiety: A retrospective study of off-label, at-home use," Frontiers in Psychiatry, 2022 SEP 28, https://doi.org/10.3389/fpsyt.2022.992624
5. "5 Things You Need To Know About Intranasal Esketamine For Depression," Reset Ketamine, 2019 MAR 4, https://www.resetketamine.com/blog/2019/3/4/5-things-you-need-to-know-about-intranasal-esketamine-for-depression
6. "FDA approves new nasal spray medication for treatment-resistant depression; available only at a certified doctor's office or clinic," U.S. Food & Drug Administration, 2019 MAR 05, https://www.fda.gov/news-events/press-announcements/fda-approves-new-nasal-spray-medication-treatment-resistant-depression-available-only-certified

Chapter 4

1. L.D. Simmler, Y. Li, L.C. Hadjas, A. Hiver, R. van Zessen, C. Lüscher, "Dual action of ketamine confines addiction liability," Nature, 2022 JUL 27, https://www.nature.com/articles/s41586-022-04993-7
2. S.E. Holmes, S.J. Finnema, M. Nakagawa, N. DellaGioia, D. Holden, K. Fowles, M. Davis, J. Ropchan, P. Emory, Y. Ye, N. Nabulsi, D. Matuskey, G.A. Angarita, R.H. Pietrzak, R.S. Duman, G. Sanacora, J.H. Krystal, R.E. Carson, I. Esterlis, "Imaging the effect of ketamine on synaptic density (SV2A) in the living brain," Molecular Psychiatry, 2022 APR, https://pubmed.ncbi.nlm.nih.gov/35165397/

Chapter 5

1. W.A. Richards, "Sacred Knowledge," New York, Columbia University Press, 2016, page 16

2. S.E. Holmes, S.J. Finnema, M. Nakagawa, N. DellaGioia, D. Holden, K. Fowles, M. Davis, J. Ropchan, P. Emory, Y. Ye, N. Nabulsi, D. Matuskey, G.A. Angarita, R.H. Pietrzak, R.S. Duman, G. Sanacora, J.H. Krystal, R.E. Carson, I. Esterlis, "Imaging the effect of ketamine on synaptic density (SV2A) in the living brain," Molecular Psychiatry, 2022 APR, https://pubmed.ncbi.nlm.nih.gov/35165397/

3. Allison C. Nugent, Kathleen E. Wills, Jessica R. Gilbert, and Carlos A. Zarate, Jr. "Synaptic potentiation and rapid antidepressant response to ketamine in treatment-resistant major depression: A replication study," Psychiatric Research: Neuroimaging, 2019 JAN, https://www.ncbi.nlm.nih.gov/pmc/articles/PMC6410365/

4. V. Hoffmann, et al, "Successful treatment of postherpetic neuralgia with oral ketamine," NIH National Library of Medicine, 1994 SEP, https://pubmed.ncbi.nlm.nih.gov/7833583/

5. H. Shanthanna, et al, "Early and effective use of ketamine for treatment of phantom limb pain," NIH National Library of Medicine, 2010 MAR-APR, https://www.ncbi.nlm.nih.gov/pmc/articles/PMC2900744/

6. L.F. Barrett, "Lisa Feldman Barrett: Pain in the brain," Massachusetts General Hospital's Center for Law, Brain & Behavior, 2015 FEB 12, https://vimeo.com/119451931

BIBLIOGRAPHY

Barrett, Lisa Feldman. How Emotions Are Made: The Secret Life of the Brain. Boston: Houghton Mifflin Harcourt, 2018

Barrett, Lisa Feldman. Seven and a Half Lessons About the Brain. Boston: Houghton Mifflin Harcourt, 2020

Fadiman, James. The Psychedelic Explorer's Guide: Safe, Therapeutic, and Sacred Journeys. Rochester, Vermont: Park Street Press, 2011

Hart, Carl. High Price: A Neuroscientist's Journey of Self-Discovery That Challenges Everything You Know About Drugs and Society. New York: HarperCollins, 2013

Hofmann, Albert. LSD: My Problem Child – Reflections on Sacred Drugs, Mysticism and Science. Santa Cruz: Multidisciplinary Association for Psychedelic Studies (MAPS), 1976

Huxley, Aldous. The Doors of Perception & Heaven and Hell. New York: HarperCollins, 2009

Jansen, Karl. Ketamine: Dreams and Realities. Santa Cruz: Multidisciplinary Association for Psychedelic Studies (MAPS), 2004

Muraresku, Brian C. The Immortality Key: The Secret History of the Religion with No Name. New York: St. Martin's Press, 2020

Richards, William A. Sacred Knowledge: Psychedelics and Religious Experiences. New York: Columbia University Press, 2016

Strassman, Rick. DMT: The Spirit Molecule. Rochester, Vermont: Park Street Press, 2001

Wolfson, Phil and Glenn Hartelius. The Ketamine Papers: Science, Therapy, and Transformation. Santa Cruz: Multidisciplinary Association for Psychedelic Studies (MAPS), 2016